International Development:
Challenges for a World in Transition

Introduction to

TRANSITIONS

Prepared for the Course Team by Simon Bromley,
Will Brown and Maureen Mackintosh

Cover photo Construction in Seoul, early 1980s.

The Open University
Walton Hall
Milton Keynes
MK7 6AA
United Kingdom

First published 2001. Reprinted 2003

Edited, designed and typeset by The Open University

Printed in the United Kingdom by Bell & Bain Ltd., Glasgow

ISBN 0 7492 3808 9

This publication forms part of an Open University course U213 *International Development: Challenges for a World in Transition*

Details of this and other Open University courses can be obtained from the Call Centre, PO Box 724, The Open University, Milton Keynes, MK7 6ZS, United Kingdom, tel. +44 (0)1908 653231, email ces-gen@open.ac.uk. Alternatively, you may visit the Open University website at http://www.open.ac.uk where you can learn more about the wide range of courses and packs offered at all levels by the Open University

If you have not already enrolled on the course and would like to purchase this or other Open University material, contact Open University Worldwide Ltd, The Berrill Building, Walton Hall, Milton Keynes MK7 6AA, United Kingdom: tel. +44 (0)1908 858785; fax +44 (0)1908 858787; email ouwenq@open.ac.uk; website http://www.ouw.co.uk

1.2

Mixed Sources
Product group from well-managed forests and other controlled sources
www.fsc.org Cert no. TT-COC-002769
© 1996 Forest Stewardship Council

The paper used in this publication contains pulp sourced from forests independently certified to the Forest Stewardship Council (FSC) principles and criteria. Chain of custody certification allows the pulp from these forests to be tracked to the end use (see www.fsc-uk.org).

Contents

Theme Introductions

Transitions is one of the five Themes you will cover while studying this course. The other four Themes are: *Poverty and Inequality*, *Technology and Knowledge*, *Displacement*, *Sustainability*.

Five weeks of study are set aside during Part 1 of U213 for these Theme Introductions, each comprising one week. You are expected to study them after you have completed your study of *Poverty and Development into the 21st Century* (Allen and Thomas, 2000; hereafter called the Course Book) and its associated audiocassettes, as directed by *Study Guide 1*. At the end of this five-week period a further week is set aside for you to complete your tutor-marked assignment TMA 03 and to make your Theme choices for Part 2 of the course.

Remember that in Part 2 you will study *three* of the five Themes in the following order:

Transitions (compulsory Theme)

Poverty and Inequality or *Technology and Knowledge*

Displacement or *Sustainability*.

The final section of *Study Guide 1* provides information that should help you make your choices. You should return to this once you have completed your study of the Theme Introductions.

Even if you are already certain which Themes you intend to study in Part 2 you should study all five Introductions in Part 1, including this one. This is because each Introduction practises skills that are relevant to other Themes and, also, we expect you to obtain a rounded view before you specialize. You may be assessed in your final examination on the learning outcomes associated with any of the Introductions. You will also be encouraged to illustrate TMA 03 with examples from a range of the Themes.

The Theme Introductions are self-contained although, as noted above, they all assume that you have completed your study of the Course Book and its associated audiocassettes. We recommend, however, that you study them during this five-week period in the following order:

First week	*Transitions*
Second week	*Poverty and Inequality*
Third week	*Technology and Knowledge*
Fourth week	*Displacement*
Fifth week	*Sustainability*

The sixth week has been set aside for completing TMA 03 and making your choices for Part 2 of the course.

Studying *Introduction to Transitions*

Some general aims of this Introduction are presented below. We also provide a checklist of learning outcomes. These are what we expect you to be able to do once you have completed the Introduction and are what you are potentially assessed upon in your TMAs and/or final examination.

The main text, which follows the aims and learning outcomes, contains activities for you to undertake. These are included to:

- engage you *actively* with the text;
- foster deeper-level study than you will be able to achieve by reading.

Typically, these activities check that you understand what is being written and can critically engage with it, and draw you into the process of developing the text argument. Do therefore attempt to do the activities *before* reading the comments that follow them. The main text also directs you from time to time to the Course Book, so make sure that you always have this to hand.

 We have used the book icon where we recommend you re-read certain pages of the Course Book.

You should aim to complete studying this Introduction in one week (about 12–14 hours of study time), which means that you should think of ways to divide up your time to work through this material. This will naturally vary between students, depending on when you have time available to work and how quickly you can go through the material. However, as a guide and an attempt to help you plan your studies, we suggest working through this Introduction in 'chunks'. We have indicated *roughly* how much time to allow for each 'chunk' in Table 1. Obviously, a more suitable division may suggest itself to you, this is presented as a suggestion only.

We recognise that there is a lot of material in what follows. However, you will return to much of this material for further study in Part 2 of the course when we look at the case of transition in relation to China, so don't worry if you cannot grasp all the details first time through.

The aims and learning outcomes that follow are for Part 1. The aims and learning outcomes for Part 2 of the *Transitions* Theme are listed in Section 6.

Aims

The aims of this Introduction are to:

- introduce the notion of transition as a structural change in the social and material organization of the economic and political life of a whole society brought about by the development of industrial capitalism;

- make an initial identification of some of the key processes involved in the transition to industrial capitalism;
- introduce some key conceptual tools from politics and economics for understanding these processes;
- illustrate some important processes of transition with reference to key historical examples.

Learning outcomes

After studying this Theme Introduction you should be able to:

1 Understand what is meant by the notion of a society-wide transition to industrial capitalism.

2 Understand some of the the key political and economic processes of transitions to industrial capitalism.

3 Understand some of the the key conceptual tools drawn from economics and politics in analysing the processes of transition to industrial capitalism.

4 Have an awareness of different historical routes to industrial capitalism.

So, *Introduction to Transitions* has aims and learning outcomes (things that you should know or be able to do by the end of it) that have a general role – they are important in their own right and have a key role in the course's aim of reframing development. However, it also seeks to establish a basis for Part 2 of the *Transitions* Theme, which will be an investigation into China's transition.

Table 1 Study timetable

	Suggested study time
Section 1 About this Theme	1 hour 15 mins
Section 2.1 Living standards, economic growth and industrialization	1 hour
Section 2.2 Accounting for intensive growth: the sources of growth and the roles of capitalism and industry	2 hours
Section 2.3 Summary of Section 2 and guide to the following section	30 mins
Section 3.1 'Making capitalism': structural change in South Korea	30 mins
Section 3.2 Markets and structural change	1 hour 30 mins
Section 3.3 Trading labour; Section 3.4 Owning, investing and trading capital; Section 3.5 Industrialization, market creation and the role of the state	1 hour 45 mins
Section 4.1 What happens when the state itself undertakes transition?	1 hour 30 mins
Section 4.2 What are states, what do they do and how do they do it?; Section 4.3 States and transition	2 hours
Section 5 Conclusion	30 mins

1 About this Theme

1.1 'Thunderous social change'

Writing about South Korea's spectacular industrialization in the post Second World War period, Alice Amsden described the process as one of 'thunderous social change' (Amsden, 1989, p.117). In the 45 years following the war the country was transformed from a traditional, semi-feudal agricultural economy into one of the leading modern industrial economies. The changes wrought on people's lives have been immense:

- Whole ways of life have been destroyed and new ones created.
- What is produced and consumed has changed out of all recognition.
- The way the country is governed has moved from feudal dynasty via military rule towards liberal democracy.

Much of this has been a very painful experience involving far-reaching social struggles, winners and losers, conflicts and crises. But South Korea is just one example out of many from the last 200 years where whole societies have been transformed. The Industrial Revolution in Britain in the nineteenth century fascinated writers such as Marx and Polanyi; the examples of the USA, Germany and Japan similarly caught the attention of contemporary observers. The turmoil involved in Russia's industrialization in the early twentieth century prompted far-reaching debates, both critical and supportive, about the changes. In fact the world we know today has been shaped to a large degree by these transformations. It is not surprising that these epoch-making convulsions – the process of becoming a modern, industrial country – remain a touchstone in almost every debate about development.

This Theme is an investigation into the processes involved when societies undergo this kind of 'transition', that is, a structural transformation in the social and material organization of the economic and political life of a whole society brought about by the development of industrial capitalism. The Theme is focused on *societies undergoing a transition to industrial capitalism*. While 'transition' broadly defined could cover a very wide range of processes – most concepts of development involve some explicit or implicit understanding of society-wide change – we are going to focus on this hugely important kind of transition. This section will explore why you need to understand the transition to industrial capitalism in a course on development. We believe there are some very compelling reasons why this is necessary. Subsequent sections will investigate key aspects of this transition:

- changes in the way economic growth occurs;
- the importance of the rise of markets and private property;
- the role of the state in such changes.

In Part 2 we will undertake a detailed investigation of the processes involved in this transition by focusing on China. While South Korea underwent a transition to industrial capitalism in the latter half of the twentieth century, China at the start of the twenty-first century is experiencing a massive and wide-ranging process of industrial change. Quite where China's transition is heading, and what the implications of this are for 'development' in general, are questions that will be debated in Part 2 of this course.

> **Transition:** Transition in this context means structural transformation in the social and material organization of the economic and political life of a whole society brought about by the development of industrial capitalism.

So what is 'industrial capitalism'? You have come across the terms 'industry' and 'capitalism' in many places in the course already and may feel that you have an idea of what is meant by them. If you are unsure, do the following activity.

Activity 1

Look up the definitions of 'industry', 'capitalism' and 'industrialization' in the Course Book. If you refer to the index, page numbers in **bold type** indicate definition boxes. There are definition boxes for each of these terms.

Comment

From these short definitions you can get an initial idea that an industrial society is one in which the economy is dominated by non-agricultural sectors of production and in which there is widespread use of advanced technology and a complex division of labour. A society is capitalist if production is carried out for sale in a market (rather than, say, for subsistence consumption) and in order to make a profit. Capitalist societies are also characterized by a particular form of class relations defined in terms of the private ownership of property and the presence of 'free' wage labour.[*]

The process of transition to industrial capitalism therefore entails the rise of these society-wide features: new kinds of production (non-agricultural, advanced technology and complex division of labour) organized in a particular kind of way (for sale in a market for profit) and involving patterns of social relations between classes structured around the ownership and non-ownership of property.

It is also implicit in the above that 'transition to industrial capitalism' encompasses two types of transition: to capitalism and to industrialization. Historically and conceptually the two are closely linked, but distinct, and in different historical cases and periods of transition we may see one before the other, or only one, or both together – something we will return to below.

Do not worry too much about the complexities of these terms just now as we return to these and other issues later. However, we do need to explain here why we want to focus on the process of transition to industrial capitalism in a course on development.

[*]In a capitalist economy wage labour is 'free' in a double sense: first, labour is freed from, that is separated from, direct rights over access to the means of production and must therefore seek waged employment in order to purchase the means of subsistence; and secondly, labour is politically free in that it is no longer politically subordinate to a superior in the way that serfs were to lords or slaves to masters.

1.2 Why do we need to know about the process of transition to industrial capitalism in a course on development?

The answer is simple. Since the transition to industrial capitalism has radically transformed the modern world, it is impossible to ignore it if we are engaged in understanding or reframing 'development'. Capitalist industrialization is itself just one version of what constitutes development. It is also a historical process that any conception of, commentary on, or analysis of, development has to say something about.

We can investigate how this is so if we refer to the ways in which the term 'development' has been used – what the word 'development' actually means. In Chapter 2 of the Course Book, Thomas presents you with three different but overlapping ways in which the term 'development' is used. These are:

1 *Development as a state of being*: that development refers to the characteristics of a society defined in terms of the conditions of its population.

2 *Development as a historical process*: that development refers to changes in society at a broad level that transforms people's lives.

3 *Development as something that is done*: that development means purposive actions by some agency, including but not limited to the state.

Of course these are not mutually exclusive ways of using the term but they do help to untangle some of the debates about development that you have encountered in Part 1 of this course. What is the relevance of the transition to industrial capitalism to these different understandings of development? Before reading how we think these issues relate to each other, you should try the following activity.

Activity 2

Keep in mind the working definition of *transition to industrial capitalism* which we discussed in our comments to Activity 1. For each of the three meanings of the term 'development' above, note how you think the transition to industrial capitalism might be relevant. You may find it useful to re-read pp.30–41 of the Course Book.

(Spend about 15 minutes on this)

Relevance of transition to industrial capitalism

Development as a state of being

Development as a historical process

Development as something that is done

Comment

Of the three meanings, development 'as a state of being' is perhaps the most obvious and common-sense idea that links the two. This is because what we mean when we talk of 'developed countries' is simply the industrial capitalist countries of the world. These countries are seen by many to represent the 'image of the future' to the developing countries. As Thomas notes in the Course Book (p.30):

> In a world dominated by advanced capitalist economies, all aspects of modern industrial society are elevated to represent the ideal of what development is trying to achieve.

An important part of this is the economic prosperity that industrial capitalism seems to deliver (for some at least). However, even if we define the 'state of being' in terms of the 'realization of human potential' then industrial capitalist countries can make a claim to represent what is 'developed' in for example providing food, jobs, education and literacy, and a minimum level of political participation. And while we might wish to consider how far these and other human needs are actually met by industrial capitalism, and at what cost, there is nevertheless room for debate. The claim has some truth in it, particularly if we contrast the human condition in industrial capitalism with that in non-industrial societies. Furthermore, in terms of the context in which we debate 'development' at the start of the twenty-first century, industrial capitalism faces few challengers when it claims to define what 'development as a state of being' means. The most obvious alternative industrialization process to that undertaken within capitalism was the 'communist' model of the Soviet Union. With its demise the field has seemingly been left open for capitalism to represent 'what development is'. The historical process whereby industrial capitalism has risen to such dominance is also central to arguments about the historical process by which development becomes possible in different parts of the world, or by which it is prevented. Furthermore, the 'state of being' of industrial capitalism is what many efforts around 'doing development' are related to, either seeking to promote industrialization or seeking to ameliorate some of the negative social consequences of transition. Either way, the process of transition maintains a central role in conceptions of what development is.

So how do societies reach such a state of being and what does this process involve? Becoming an industrial capitalist society entails precisely a transition: a structural change across the whole of society. But what do we mean by 'structural change'? The Course Book (p.189) provides us with a definition of *structure* as:

> ... the pattern or framework of relationships between social institutions, such as markets, families, classes and political factions. It includes rules of behaviour associated, for example, with moral norms and hierarchies.

Structural change therefore entails changes in these patterns of relationships across the whole society. In *Introduction to Transitions* we will explore structural change in:

- the economy, in what is produced and how the economy grows;
- social relations and in particular the relations between labour, capital and the role of markets and property;
- politics, particularly in relations between the state and society.

We need to note one further thing. We mentioned above that 'transition to industrial capitalism' actually entails two distinct transitions. Some of the structural changes we will note (changes in what is produced, for example) may be more obviously related to the 'industrialization' aspect of transition while others (changes in property relations, for example) may be more central to the 'capitalist' transition. In many countries the transition to capitalism and industrialization have been very closely bound up with each other, but in some communist countries industrialization has occurred *without* a transition to capitalism. We will note in the sections below how the transition to capitalism was under way well before industrialization in Britain. In the Soviet Union most of the industrialization process occurred under communism and only since the late 1980s has a transition to capitalism recommenced. This distinction is important for analysing historical examples of transition, and will be important when we come to analyse what kind of transition is under way in China in Part 2. However, it is also important to note this distinction because much contemporary literature talks of transition in this latter, more specific, sense – the political and economic transition to capitalism in the former communist countries following the fall of the Berlin Wall in 1989. As we have noted, we have a somewhat broader view of transition than some of this contemporary literature, although key aspects of the processes involved may be common to both.

1.3 Summary of Section 1 and guide to the following sections

Let us summarize the claims that we have made so far and indicate how we will take forward your understanding of the *transition to industrial capitalism*.

Summary of Section 1
We have argued that the process of transition – understood as a structural change in the social and material economic and political organization of society – towards industrial capitalism is one that is at the heart of almost any attempt to tackle the question of what we mean by development, and it is the central reference point in theoretical debates about development. For some, industrial capitalism *is* development: it is the desirable developed state to be aimed for, it is the historical process that development is about and it is the transition in society that actions to 'do' development are aimed at. However, whatever your standpoint in debates about development, transition is a structural transformation in society as a whole that cannot be ignored if you are to engage properly with the task of reframing development.

Looking forward

So how are we going to develop our understanding of what this transition involves?

Industrialization has for many delivered increasing standards of living – indeed this is one of the reasons why it is such a central process for reframing development. But this is in turn based on changes in the kind of economic growth that takes place, which is in turn based on structural changes in the economy – that is *what is produced and how*. Section 2 will look at these issues. You should already have some idea of where and when industrialization has taken place. Section 2 will also tackle this issue. The process of capitalist industrialization also involves fundamental changes in the way that society as a whole, and especially the economy, is organized. In particular:

■ markets become a central, if not dominant, mechanism in the economy;

■ the way that labour is incorporated into the economy is fundamentally altered;

■ investment becomes a key feature of economies;

■ property relations are revolutionized.

All of these processes are introduced in Section 3. Finally, these changes also entail changes in the role of the state which is often a key agency in pushing forward structural changes in other parts of society. But this in turn implies a changed relationship between the state and society. Section 4 will focus on the state, its actions, and its relationship to society.

All of this may sound daunting – we are after all talking about epoch-making changes in society! We will therefore proceed carefully through these different dimensions of transition. However, this will mean that we need to define and use some key concepts from politics and economics. Some of these may be familiar to you, others less so. Thus, while the following sections will deal with the processes involved – changes in the kind of economic growth, structural changes in the economy and the actions and relationship of the state to society – you will also need to develop your understanding of the key concepts involved. Among those you will take a close look at are: economic growth, productivity, industrialization, markets, property, capital, states, power and legitimation. All of these are key concepts for understanding many aspects of development, however it is conceived. They are also vital to understanding transition to industrial capitalism and will be deployed when we come to the case study of China, which is the main focus of Part 2. The activities within the text are designed to ensure that you have a grasp of these concepts.

Finally, in covering these issues, we will make some fairly substantial claims and at times have to be more general than we would ideally like to be. At this stage in the course you should already be aware that most aspects of international development are debated and open to challenge – and transition to industrial capitalism is no different. You will no doubt feel that you want to challenge some of what is being said here. We would encourage you to do so and at times you will be explicitly invited to do so.

2 Growth, productivity and industrialization

We noted in Section 1 that transition to industrial capitalism is closely associated with notions of what 'being developed' means. A central, though not only, reason for this is to do with the increased standards of living that industrial capitalism can deliver. But how is this so? Why, despite all the many negative consequences of transition (the social dislocation, harsh working conditions and so on), are high standards of living associated with the rise of industrial capitalism? The main purpose of this section is to explore why this is so and, in particular, to look at how the nature of economic growth changes with the transition to industrial capitalism. Along the way we will note the structural changes in the economy which industrialization brings and look at the relationship between 'industry' and 'capitalism' that lies behind these changes.

2.1 Living standards, economic growth and industrialization

Let us begin by considering what living standards were like before industrialization. Before the eighteenth century, 75–80% of the working population in Europe were employed on the land; in the non-European world the proportion was even higher, perhaps 85–90%. In the major civilizations of Europe and Asia based on settled agriculture and domesticated animals, with literacy, coinage, metals and cities, only about 10% of the population was urban. Life expectancy at birth was perhaps 20–35 years. Anywhere between one-fifth and one-half of all newborn infants died before they reached their first birthday. These patterns had remained basically unchanged since the spread and consolidation of the agricultural revolution several thousands of years before. As the economic historian, Carlo Cipolla, pointed out:

> In all agricultural societies of our past we find that … the great mass of people can hardly afford to satisfy anything but the more elementary needs … [M]ost of the available resources are employed in agriculture, textile manufacture and building … [Agriculture] absorbs the greatest quota of capital and labour … [It] represents the pivotal point around which all other activities tend to revolve.
>
> (Cipolla, 1965, p.62)

Most of the working population most of the time were employed in feeding themselves and providing limited clothing, shelter and other basic necessities. This is not to say that there was never economic growth in agricultural societies, but it tended to take the form of increases in output associated with increases in population as more land was taken into cultivation, rather than increases in output per worker, so that the standard of living advanced very slowly, if at all. Often the rate of population increase would run ahead of economic growth and average living standards would fall. Moreover, survival within agricultural societies was perpetually under threat from recurrent crop failures and epidemic diseases, often as a result of warfare. In Europe it was not until the seventeenth century that famine ceased to be an ever-present threat.

Measuring and understanding economic growth

One of the ways we can characterize the increase in living standards during industrialization is to draw a distinction between *extensive growth* and *intensive growth*. A straightforward answer to the question 'what is economic growth?' is that it is an increase in the level of output of an economy. But as we noted above, if the population is also increasing, a rise in the amount produced might *not* translate into more output per person. It is therefore often useful to measure economic growth per head (often referred to as *per capita*). We can then say an economy is growing when it produces more output for each person, year on year. Sometimes historians and economists distinguish between extensive and intensive growth to make this point (Jones, 1988). In what follows, we will use the terms:

- *extensive growth* to refer to an increase in output matched by a growing population, such that output per head is stationary;
- *intensive growth* to refer to a situation of rising per capita output, often combined with a rise in the population growth rate as well.

*GDP per capita is often used as an indicator of the standard of living, as we have done in this text. However, we have noted already in this course some of the problems involved in using measurements like GDP and GNP (gross national product). You might as a result want to question their use here, or return to the discussion in Chapter 1 of the Course Book on the relationship between GNP and poverty.

Gross domestic product (GDP) measures the aggregate value of the goods and services produced by the economy during a year. GDP per capita* is therefore an economy's GDP divided by its population. An alternative measure would be GDP per worker. GDP per capita tells us how much output is available per person whereas GDP per worker tells us how much output is produced per worker. All of these measures relate to the level of output (per capita or per worker). They do *not* tell us anything about how fast or slowly the economy is growing. For that we need to measure the *rate of growth*.

What is a growth rate? The easiest way to think about the growth rate of some variable (output, population, etc.) is in terms of percentage changes. For example, if the GDP of an economy in year zero is $100 billion and in year one it is $102 billion, then the annual growth rate is 2%. Output has increased by $2bn from a base of $100bn.

Activity 3

Suppose the growth rate stays constant at 2%. What will the output be in year two?

Comment

It will be $104.04bn.

Remember that per cent (symbolized by %) means 'out of a hundred', so to say that we have an annual growth rate of 2% is saying that output increases to $102bn (100 + 2) out of (or from a base of) $100bn, that is output each year is 102% of the previous year.

To get 102% from a base of 100 is straightforward. But how do we calculate 102% of something when our starting point is not $100bn but $102bn? The answer is that we treat our starting point as if it were 100% and proceed in exactly the same way: that is, we divide by 100 to give us 1% of our starting point and multiply by 102 to give us 102%.

For year one we had

$$\frac{\$100bn}{100} \times 102 = \$102bn$$

So in year two we treat the $102bn as if it were 100% and proceed as follows:

$$\frac{\$102bn}{100} \times 102 = \$104.04bn$$

Now do this for the following year:

$$\frac{\$104.04bn}{100} \times 102 = \$106.12bn$$

And so on. Calculate one more year and check your answer in Table 2.1.

Finally, what are the consequences of sustaining a growth rate of output per head of, say, 5% as opposed to 2% year after year? The effects are dramatic because of 'compounding'. Activity 3 above illustrated this idea: the 2% growth rate in year two applies not only to the original $100bn, but also to the additional $2bn – that is, it *compounds* the earlier year's growth. The effects are dramatic. Table 2.1 gives some figures for output at 2% growth rate and 5% growth rate (check that you understand the calculations).

Table 2.1 The effect of different constant growth rates on level of output

Year	Output at 2% growth rate ($bn)	Output at 5% growth rate ($bn)
0	100.00	100.00
1	102.00	105.00
2	104.04	110.25
3	106.12	115.76
4	108.24	121.55
5	110.41	127.63
10	121.90	162.89
20	148.59	265.33
35	199.99	551.60

Figure 2.1 The dramatic effect over time of a higher constant growth rate.

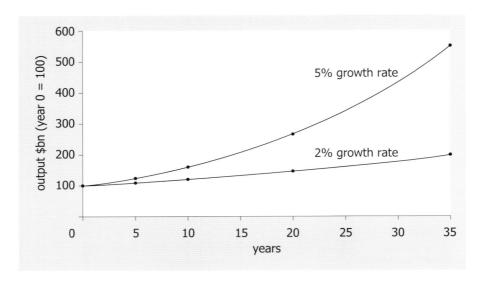

Figure 2.1 illustrates graphically the effects of different constant growth rates on the level of output: notice how the country with the 5% growth rate moves further and further ahead of the one with a 2% growth rate.

The important point to notice in the columns in Table 2.1 above is that while in each case the growth rate is constant (at 2% or 5% a year), the *size* of the increase in output gets bigger each year. This can be seen clearly in Figure 2.1. While the percentage change remains the same, the absolute size of the increase gets ever larger. Compounding in this way can produce dramatic results in the standard of living, even with quite small growth rates (see Box 2.1).

Box 2.1 Growth rates and the long-run standard of living

To help you get an intuitive sense of the importance of thinking about the effects of compounding on the level of output, a useful, albeit rough, rule of thumb is: *the number of years needed to double the standard of living is 70 divided by the percentage growth rate of output per head.* (There is a mathematical reason why the figure 70 is used but we don't need worry about this here.) So with a growth rate per head of 2% it takes about 35 years to double the living standards; with a growth rate per head of 5% it takes about 14 years to double the living standards. Prior to the onset of industrialization these growth rates are typically between 0.1% and 0.2%, implying a doubling period ranging from 350 to 700 years! So, although a growth rate of per capita output of, say, 2% might not sound very large, it implies more than a doubling of real living standards in an average lifetime.

Once industrialization began, in the late eighteenth and early nineteenth centuries in Europe, the standard or level of living changed rapidly. The onset of industrialization was associated with a rise in the rate of economic growth and over time the cumulative impact of this increase on levels of output per capita has been spectacular. Angus Maddison estimates that:

> ... since 1820 the advanced capitalist countries have increased their total product seventyfold and now account for half of world GDP. Their real per capita income is now fourteen times what it was in 1820, and six times as high as the average for the rest of the world.
>
> (Maddison, 1991, p.1)

Table 2.2 shows the rates of growth of GDP per capita of selected regions of the world from the 1820s until 1989.

Activity 4

In which period were per capita growth rates the highest for each of the regions listed in Table 2.2?

Comment

As you can see from Table 2.2, by 1820 Europe already registered higher rates of growth than the rest of the world. However, as industrialization spreads internationally in the late nineteenth and twentieth centuries, growth rates increase in the other regions. The post-war era (1950–73) shows the highest growth rates for all areas except Asia, which sees its growth accelerate even further in the 1973–89 period. As Chapter 13 of the Course Book noted, the post-war period up until the 1970s was one of sustained high growth across the world and this seems to be reflected in the table. Furthermore, the process of decolonization and the increase in the numbers of developing countries actively pursuing industrialization may have also contributed to higher growth rates.

Table 2.2 Rates of growth of GDP per capita, 1820–1989 (annual averages)

	1820–1870	*1870–1913*	*1913–1950*	*1950–1973*	*1973–1989*
European capitalist core and its new world offshoots[a]	0.9	1.4	1.2	3.5	2.1
European periphery[b]	0.6	1.0	1.1	4.3	1.7
Latin America[c]	0.3	1.1	1.4	2.5	0.6
Asia[d]	0.1	0.6	−0.1	3.5	4.2
Africa[e]	n.a.	n.a.	1.2	1.9	−0.3

[a]Austria, Belgium, Denmark, Finland, France, Germany, Italy, Netherlands, Norway, Sweden, UK, Australia, Canada, United States.

[b]Czechoslovakia, Greece, Hungary, Ireland, Portugal, Spain, Soviet Union.

[c]Argentina, Brazil, Chile, Colombia, Mexico, Peru.

[d]Bangladesh, China, India, Indonesia, Japan, Korea, Pakistan, Taiwan, Thailand.

[e]Cote d'Ivoire, Ghana, Kenya, Morocco, Nigeria, South Africa, Tanzania.

n.a. = data not available.

Source: adapted from Maddison, A. (1994) 'Explaining the economic performance of nations, 1820–1989', in Baumol, W.J., Nelson, R.R. and Wolff, E.N. (eds), *Convergence of Productivity: cross-national studies and historical evidence*, Oxford University Press, New York, pp.26–27, table 2.2.

Indeed, total world output in the 1990s was some 40 times larger than in the 1820s. Not only has world output exploded since the beginnings of industrialization but so also has the world's population: in the eighteenth century the total population is estimated as having been 650–850 million; it is now over 6 billion (thousand millions). Worldwide, people now live much longer and healthier lives and, in the high-income industrial societies, average life expectancy is in the 70s and 80s, compared with perhaps 20–35 years in the era of agrarianism.

However, we should note at this stage that despite the spread of industrialization after 1950 and its development outside Europe and the areas of European settlement, the distribution of industrial production on a worldwide basis has been an extremely uneven and unequal process. By the end of the twentieth century, some two hundred years after the process began, three countries – the USA, Japan and Germany – accounted for 60% of world manufactured output.

- The rich countries who make up the Organization for Economic Co-operation and Development (OECD) accounted for around four-fifths of the total world manufacturing output (with a combined population of less than one-fifth of the world total).

- The rest of the world – the developing countries with four-fifths of the world's population – produced only one-fifth of world manufacturing output, most of which was concentrated in a small number of developing economies, especially in East Asia.

Nevertheless, other parts of the world did begin to join the pattern of intensive growth. Table 2.3 shows the growth of real output per capita for selected countries either side of what it calls their 'turning point', defined as the date 'after which living levels begin to advance at a previously unprecedented pace' (Easterlin, 2000, p.10).

Table 2.3 Growth rate of real GDP per capita in the half century before and after its turning point in six countries (average annual growth rate, %)

	Approximate date of turning point	*GDP per capita at turning point (1990 dollars)*	*Growth rate of GDP per capita (% per year)*		*Change in growth rate*
			Before turning point	*After turning point*	
United Kingdom	1820	1756	0.4	1.3	
France	1820	1218	0.3	0.9	
Sweden	1850	1289	0.2	1.3	
Japan	1870	741	0.1	1.7	
Brazil	1900	737	0.1	1.7	
India	1945	663	0.1	1.7	

Source: Easterlin, R.A. (2000) 'The worldwide standard of living since 1800', *The Journal of Economic Perspectives*, vol.14, no.1, Winter 2000, p.10, table 2.

Activity 5

Complete the final column in Table 2.3 by calculating the change in growth rate for each of the countries listed. (Hint: subtract *Before turning point* from *After turning point*.)

What patterns can you identify in Table 2.3? (Hint: look at the columns *GDP per capita at turning point* and *Change in growth rate*.)

(Spend about 15 minutes on this)

Comment

As you can see from Table 2.3, it is possible to identify substantial increases in the per capita growth rates for each of the countries. This enables us to define the turning point as *the period after which significant intensive growth characterizes the overall performance of the economy.* However, there is a trend evident whereby the later industrializers (Japan, Brazil and India) show the largest changes in growth rates. This may have something to do with late industrialization which historically has been more rapid, concentrated and 'forced' than the slower and more gradual move from extensive to intensive growth evident in, for example, Britain. You should also note the differences in starting point given in the second column (GDP per capita at turning point). The three later industrializers all had a much lower GDP per capita at their turning point which may have a bearing on the potential for the initial very high rates of growth afterwards.

Another way of illustrating this shift to intensive growth is represented in Figure 2.2 (source: IMF 2000). In the graph you can see that while population increased substantially in the twentieth century, world GDP increased proportionally much more. If you look at the bar chart the compounding effects of significant intensive growth for levels of output are clear from the late nineteenth century onwards, and especially after 1950.

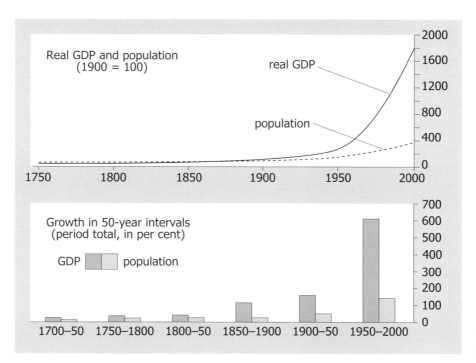

Figure 2.2 World GDP and population since 1750.

Structural change: the decline of agriculture and the rise of industry and services

Another fundamental feature of intensive growth is that it involves a sustained fall of the share of agriculture in output and employment in the economy as a whole. Indeed, the much richer, larger population of the early twenty-first century is sustained by a much smaller share of the population working on the land. In the high-income capitalist countries where these changes have gone furthest, the share of the population employed on the land has fallen dramatically, to well under 5% of the working population in most cases, and often as low as 2% or less. On the *supply* side, the output produced per worker has increased in the agricultural sector so that a smaller share of the labour force is needed to feed the population (and food is also imported). On the *demand* side, as incomes rise consumers have come to spend a smaller share of their total income on agricultural goods. These changes released labour from agricultural production and allowed employment in other sectors of the economy – industry and services – to grow.

More generally, an increase in productivity (Box 2.2) across the economy as a whole is a central feature of intensive economic growth. This has been implicit in what we have said already, since we have defined intensive growth as increases in output per capita. If we assume that a constant share of the population is employed, then an increase in output per capita is also an increase in output per worker. That is, *intensive growth implies a growth in labour productivity*.

Box 2.2 Productivity
Production systems use factors of production – such as labour with different skills, and capital inputs such as machines – to produce outputs from raw materials and manufactured inputs. If the amounts of labour and capital increase, then we would expect output to increase: for example output may rise because there is an increase in the proportion of the population employed. However, if output rises faster than we would expect it to, from the observed increase in capital and labour employed, then productivity is rising. We can measure changes in labour productivity as changes in output per worker. But economists are particularly interested in measuring changes in 'total factor productivity': that is, the increase in output not explained by increases in labour and capital inputs. An increase in total factor productivity is generally attributed to technical change: that is, to changes in the methods of production and in the way production is organized.

Later we will discuss what causes productivity to increase. But for now we will consider further our argument that *intensive* growth involves among other things a continual improvement in labour productivity (output per worker). One benefit of viewing economic growth in terms of the growth of labour productivity is that it enables us to see that growth not only raises living standards but also allows resources (in this case, labour) to be reallocated to new kinds of activities. Intensive economic growth thus not only delivers more of the same but also changes the *structure* of the economy: patterns of employment and output change dramatically, such that people are performing different kinds of productive activity, producing a different (expanding) range of goods and services. They also do this under changed conditions of work as we shall see in Section 3 below. As we noted in Section 1, structural change is central to our understanding of transition. Here we can see that one aspect of the transition to industrial capitalism is the structural change in the relationship between different parts of the economy.

Table 2.4[*] illustrates this process of structural change for the three leading economies since the advent of sustained intensive growth. In the eighteenth century the Netherlands was the lead economy, followed by Britain in the nineteenth century and the United States in the twentieth century.

[*]Table 2.4 uses the concept of 'employment' to mean not just wage labour, but the work people are doing more generally, whether they are paid a wage or whether, for example, they work on their own farms or in their own workshops.

Table 2.4 Employment structure in the lead countries, 1700–1989 (% of total employment)

	Netherlands	UK	USA
1700			
Agriculture	40	56	n.a.
Industry	33	22	n.a.
Services	27	22	n.a.
1820			
Agriculture	n.a.	40	n.a.
Industry	n.a.	32	n.a.
Services	n.a.	28	n.a.
1890			
Agriculture	33	16	39
Industry	31	44	27
Services	36	40	34
1989			
Agriculture	5	2	3
Industry	26	29	26
Services	69	69	71

n.a. = data not available.

Source: Maddison, A. (1991) *Dynamic Forces in Capitalist Development: a long-run comparative view*, Oxford University Press, Oxford, p.32, table 2.1.

So, to summarize what we have covered so far:

- Historically, the transition to industrial capitalism has delivered rising standards of living.
- This is based on a shift from extensive growth to intensive growth.
- This in turn implies structural changes in the economy, in particular in the movement of labour and consumption away from agriculture.

We now need to ask what drives intensive growth and the associated structural change in the economy.

2.2 Accounting for intensive growth: the sources of growth and the roles of capitalism and industry

There is more than one way of thinking about the causes of intensive growth. The economic historian, Angus Maddison, says that:

> In assessing the nature of capitalist performance, one can conduct the causal analysis at two levels – 'ultimate' and 'proximate'.
>
> (Maddison, 1991, p.10)

By the 'ultimate' causes Maddison means all those background changes in the nature of the economy, society and culture, and the state, including the international context, which resulted in new kinds of economic growth and change. 'Proximate' causes, according to Maddison, include the kinds of variables that are the particular subject of economic theory: variables that economists seek to define and measure. There are thus two different (though we hope complementary) ways of answering the question 'What drives intensive growth?'

Taking the proximate causes first, one can follow the lead of economists and economic historians and ask about the sources of economic growth. Did growth rates rise because more inputs were mobilized into the economy – more labour by increasing the share of the population in employment and more capital by diverting resources from current consumption to increase future production? Or did growth rates increase because advances in technology and organization allowed given inputs to be used more efficiently: that is, more productively? Or was it some combination of these factors? What is known as 'growth accounting' is an attempt to answer these kinds of question. The details of growth accounting are complex but the basic idea is simple, and Box 2.2 above discussing *productivity* above draws on it. Growth accounting starts by measuring the rate of growth of output of an economy, and the rates of growth of its various inputs. The calculation then attributes part of the observed output growth to the change in inputs, and measures the residual as the increase in total factor productivity. This is therefore a measure of the increased efficiency (productivity) with which the inputs are converted into outputs and, as Box 2.2 notes, is often understood as a measure of the rate of technical progress or innovation. Growth accounting thus sets out to determine the relative contribution to observed increases in output of the various potential sources of growth.

Intensive growth in an industrial capitalist economy might arise for one or all of the following reasons:

1 The economy might use its available labour input more efficiently as a result of the development of an increasingly specialized division of labour on the basis of an expansion of markets.

2 The labour might become more skilled as a result of experience, education and training.

3 The economy might set aside resources from current consumption and invest in the accumulation of capital to build up the amount of tools, machinery and other resources that workers can use in future production.

4 There may be technological and organizational innovations which enable given quantities of labour or capital to be used more efficiently.

5 The structure of incentives and constraints that reward economic actors (firms, workers, etc.) might change in ways that encourage greater efficiency.

Once the sources of growth have been identified, one can ask what kinds of changes might account for the various sources. Suppose, for example, that the results of growth accounting during a particular period of economic growth showed that the main sources were the growth of capital inputs resulting from capital accumulation and the rate of technical progress. According to Maddison this is the general picture for capitalist development:

> The most striking characteristic of capitalist performance has been a sustained upward thrust in productivity and real income per head, which was achieved by a combination of innovation and accumulation.
>
> (Maddison, 1991, p.5)

We would still be left with the 'ultimate' question 'Why does capitalism lead to an increase in the accumulation of capital and innovation?' Growth accounting does *not* answer this question. The question of how and why industrial capitalism results in intensive growth based on the accumulation of capital and technical progress, rather than the more extensive mobilization of labour inputs typical of pre-capitalist agrarian economies, remains to be explained after we have identified the proximate sources of growth.

At different times different analysts of industrial capitalism have highlighted the role of different factors in generating intensive growth. Perhaps this reflects the relative importance of different causes at different times and in different places, for there is no reason to suppose that there is a single, fixed set of causes that operate in the same way for all times and all places. Patterns of growth seem to be historically and geographically varied.

For example:

- The Scottish economist and philosopher, Adam Smith (1723–90), gave a central place to the development of the division of labour and the role of specialization (and within this to the increasing skills of labour) made possible by the expansion of markets.

- Karl Marx (1818–83) emphasized the importance of the accumulation of capital and the introduction of machinery into the production process.

- The Austrian economist, Joseph Schumpeter (1883–1950), stressed the role of technical and organizational progress.

All these writers saw the changes in the incentive structure associated with the development of capitalism as a crucial part of the process of intensive economic growth.

The division of labour and the growth of labour productivity

In agricultural economies intensive economic growth involving a sustained rise in living standards, perhaps combined with a rising population, was not only comparatively rare but also susceptible to periodic set-backs and large-scale regressions. Nevertheless, intensive economic growth began in what were essentially agrarian economies well before the onset of the Industrial Revolution. Indeed, from the middle of the sixteenth century through to the beginning of the nineteenth century, the British *agrarian* economy moved ahead of the other European economies at the same time as Europe was forging ahead of the rest of the world. We can see this by looking at the structure of employment. For example by 1800 in England 'only about 40% of the adult male labour force worked in agriculture' compared with 60–80% in other European countries (Wrigley, 1988, p.12).

As we have just seen, intensive growth requires an increase in labour productivity – the amount produced per worker. Writing towards the end of the period of agrarian capitalism, but before the Industrial Revolution had really got under way, Adam Smith attributed this economic growth to the emergence of a commercial society in which economic activity was organized by markets and where property rights and contracts were securely protected by law and the state. Under these circumstances, Smith argued that the productivity of labour could be increased by an advancing division of labour.[*]

*You have come across division of labour in the Course Book, ch.5, p.116.

Technological and organizational changes linked to a growing division of labour and level of specialization within and between productive units, combined with an expansion of trade and markets, would allow labour to be used with ever greater efficiency (Box 2.3). Smith was also aware that the accumulation of capital played a role in the growth process but:

> ... he treats capital mainly as a stock which can be increased in per capita terms to make it possible to use more complex methods of production rather than new techniques.
>
> (Maddison, 1991, p.16)

Box 2.3 Adam Smith's theory of economic growth

'The annual labour of every nation is the fund which originally supplies it with all the necessaries and conveniences of life which it annually consumes, and which consist always, either in the immediate produce of that labour, or in what is purchased with that produce from other nations. According therefore, as this produce, or what is purchased with it, bears a greater or smaller proportion to the number of those who are to consume it, the nation will be better or worse supplied with all the necessaries and conveniences for which it has occasion. But this proportion must in every nation be regulated by two different circumstances; first, by the skill, dexterity, and judgement with which its labour is generally applied; and, secondly, by the proportion between the number of those who are employed in useful labour, and that of those who are not so employed ... The greatest improvement in the productive powers of labour, and the greater part of the skill, dexterity, and judgement with which it is in any where directed, or applied, seem to have been the effects of the division of labour ... This division of labour ... is the necessary, though very slow and gradual consequence of a certain propensity in human nature which has in view no such extensive utility; the propensity to truck, barter, and exchange one thing for another ... As it is the power of exchanging that gives occasion to the division of labour, so the extent of this division must always be limited by the extent of that power, or, in other words, by the extent of the market ... [A]s labour comes to be more and more divided ... a variety of new machines come to be invented for facilitating and abridging those operations.'

(Smith, 1993, *An Inquiry into the Natures and Causes of the Wealth of Nations*, pp.8, 11, 21, 26, 160)

Activity 6

Go back to Chapter 2 of the Course Book by Thomas and re-read Section 2.3. What explanation does the chapter offer for the dynamics of capitalist growth?

(Spend about 15 minutes on this)

Comment

Thomas discusses those views which see market competition as the main force creating economic growth under capitalism, since competition encourages entrepreneurs to invest (or accumulate) a proportion of their profits in order to expand the size of their business and so outgrow their rivals, and to innovate, that is to devise new and better technologies and ways of organizing production. Thomas says that both of these activities increase labour productivity (output per worker) and require investment from savings, or 'surplus accumulation'. However, Thomas notes that while investment is a necessary condition for growth and innovation, it is not sufficient: 'although there can be no economic growth without investment, by itself investment is not sufficient to guarantee growth'. Thomas also links economic growth to the idea of industrialization:

growth and innovation involve precisely the development of a more complex social and technical division of labour and the adoption of more advanced technologies that are the defining features of industrialization (see also the discussion of the division of labour in Chapter 5 of the Course Book, especially Section 5.2).

Notice also that Thomas draws attention to the fact that while industrial capitalism may become an engine of economic growth once established, there is an argument between those who follow Adam Smith in seeing markets as naturally developing wherever they are 'free from outside regulation' and others, most notably Karl Polanyi, who argue that markets have to be created and sustained by political organization and power. (We will return to this debate in Sections 3 and 4 below.)

This suggests that we have two related candidates for the 'ultimate' sources of intensive growth – capitalism and industrialization – and we now consider these in turn.

Intensive economic growth and the rise of capitalism

In explaining the ultimate origin of intensive economic growth, some writers put the emphasis on the rise of capitalism in Western Europe as the key historical departure. For this argument to be sustained it is first necessary to establish that intensive growth was first seen in Western Europe. Although some writers have argued that Sung China (between the tenth and thirteenth centuries) and Tokugawa Japan (in the eighteenth and nineteenth centuries) experienced intensive growth (Jones, 1988), others, for example Angus Maddison, are sceptical, denying that these were at all comparable to Western Europe in the nineteenth century.

Maddison has estimated the annual average growth rates for population and per capita output for the advanced capitalist countries over the last 1500 years. His results are shown in Table 2.5 below.

Table 2.5 Long-run rate of growth of population and per capita output

	Annual average growth rate (%)	
	Population	Per capita output
Agrarianism (500–1500)	0.1	0.0
Advancing agrarianism (1500–1700)	0.2	0.1
Merchant capitalism (1700–1820)	0.4	0.2
Capitalism (1820–1980)	0.9	1.6

Source: Maddison, A. (1982) *Phases of Capitalist Development*, Oxford University Press, New York, p.6, table 1.2.

Activity 7

Using Table 2.5, identify in which period:

(a) there was extensive growth only;

(b) intensive growth starts;

(c) intensive growth takes off.

(Spend 10 minutes on this)

Comment

You should have noted that what Maddison calls the period of advancing agrarianism and merchant capitalism (the sixteenth and seventeenth centuries) saw the modest beginning of intensive growth as compared with the essentially low-level extensive growth of the agrarian period. These dates coincide roughly with the period of the transition to agrarian capitalism in Britain and, then, in much of the rest of north-west Europe. But the really explosive breakthrough into intensive growth dates from the nineteenth century, again first in Britain and then in much of the rest of Europe and some of the areas of European conquest and settlement in other parts of the world (most notably, North America). On this view, it is the rise of capitalism in Western Europe which kick-starts the spread of intensive economic growth. This is a view shared by Henry Bernstein writing in the Course Book (ch.11).

As far as the question of development is concerned, one very important consequence of the uneven advent of intensive economic growth has been the resulting pattern of inequality on a worldwide scale. Prior to the 1800s, there was a rough parity in standards of living between the major agrarian civilizations of the world. In 1750, for example, around three-quarters of the world's total population was to be found in China, India, Europe, Japan and the Ottoman Empire – and in the preceding several centuries average living standards in these regions were broadly comparable. According to the economic historian, Paul Bairoch:

> … before the Industrial Revolution the income differential between the poorest and the richest country was certainly smaller than 1 to 2 and probably of the order of only 1 to 1.5 … [I]f instead of countries we refer to broader geographic entities such as Western Europe, India, pre-Columbian America, Africa or China, the differential was probably even smaller, of the order of 1.0 to 1.3 or even less.

> (Bairoch, 1993, p.104)

For reasons that continue to be much debated, sometime around 1500 according to Maddison and certainly by the late eighteenth century, rates of economic growth in Western Europe began to forge ahead of the other major civilizations in China, India and the Ottoman Empire. (The pre-Columbian civilizations in South America were effectively destroyed by European conquest.) The consequences for the relative fortunes of different regions were dramatic as we can see by comparing, for example, the long-run fortunes of Western Europe and China. Table 2.6 below gives some rough estimates for the comparative performance of Western Europe (and its offshoots[a]) and China, 1400–1989.

Table 2.6 Comparative performance of Western Europe (and its offshoots[a]) and China, 1400–1989

Year	GDP per capita (dollars at 1985 prices)		Population (millions)	
	Western Europe and offshoots[a]	China	Western Europe and offshoots[a]	China
1400	430	500	43	74
1820	1034	500	122	342
1950	4902	454	412	547
1989	14 413	2361	587	1120

[a]For the purposes of this comparison, the 'offshoots' are Australia, Canada and the United States.

Source: Maddison, A. (1991) *Dynamic Forces in Capitalist Development: a long-run comparative view*, Oxford University Press, Oxford, p.10, table 1.3.

Activity 8

Compare the GDP per capita and population in Western Europe and its offshoots and China. Which of the following statements are correct?

(a) GDP per capita of Western Europe and its offshoots has always been greater than China's GDP.

(b) By 1820 GDP per capita of Western Europe and its offshoots was more than double China's GDP per capita.

(c) Between 1820 and 1950 GDP per capita of Western Europe and its offshoots increased almost fivefold.

(d) Between 1820 and 1950 China's GDP per capita increased dramatically.

(e) The population of Western Europe and its offshoots was greater than the population of China between 1400 and 1950.

(Spend about 15 minutes on this)

Comment

As you will probably have noted:

Statement (a) is false although GDP per capita for the two regions were very close in 1400.

Statements (b) and (c) are true and reflect the fact that while living standards in China remained static, in Western Europe and its offshoots they had forged ahead. Up until 1820 population growth in China was much higher than in Western Europe and its offshoots, suggesting that while China's growth remained extensive, Western Europe and its offshoots were entering an era of intensive growth.

Statement (d) is false – in fact by 1950, while living standards in Western Europe and its offshoots had increased nearly fivefold on their 1820 levels, those in China regressed slightly. In this period, the rate of population growth was much higher in Europe and its offshoots than in China (although statement (e) is still false as China has a larger population throughout). This is consistent with continued intensive growth in Western Europe and its offshoots, supporting an expanding population. If Maddison's data are reliable, China, by contrast, experienced a fall in living standards as the population increased slightly more rapidly than output. Finally, in the second half of the twentieth century, China began to close the gap in living standards with Western Europe and its offshoots (their GDP per capita was 10.8 times that of China in 1950 but had fallen to 6.1 by 1989), and its population once again expanded rapidly (doubling) while that of Western Europe and its offshoots now increased much more slowly than before. Did this signal that China was beginning to enter the kind of intensive growth that Western Europe and its offshoots embarked upon after the 1820s?

If we are to follow Adam Smith, Karl Marx and more recent analysts like Angus Maddison, it is the shift to agrarian capitalism in Western Europe and its offshoots that establishes a path of intensive growth, a path that China (and many other developing countries) only embark on after 1950, if then. But is capitalism the whole answer? After all, China did not have a capitalist economy after 1950. Like the Soviet Union (see Section 4 below) it had a communist economic system and both countries have experienced intensive growth without capitalism. What else might contribute to intensive growth in an economy over time? How does an industrial revolution change the prospects for such growth? These are questions we will look at next.

Intensive growth and industrial revolutions*

We have seen that intensive growth within agrarian capitalism not only raised per capita living standards and supported a rapidly expanding population but also allowed labour to move out of agricultural production into other activities. We have also seen that economic growth presupposes investment, or the accumulation of capital. However, for some writers, fundamental features of industrialization are key to explaining how intensive growth accelerated (note that as shown in Tables 2.5 and 2.6 above, once industrialization takes hold in Western Europe from 1820, growth rates increase most markedly). So what is it about industrialization, as distinct from capitalism, that is so important to growth? Is industrialization the ultimate cause of intensive growth?

Broadly speaking, there are three different, if overlapping, ways of characterizing industrial revolutions.

1   Industrial revolution can be described in terms of the changing *social framework* of the economy as a whole: it involved the emergence of private property in the means of production, competitive markets for goods, and the creation of a 'free' labour force – free of, or from, ties to the means of subsistence on the land and free to work for those with property. This is what Adam Smith had in mind when he spoke of 'commercial society' and what Marx called capitalist 'relations of production'. This notion of an industrial revolution is also central to Polanyi's conception of the market economy in *The Great Transformation*. In this sense, 'industrial revolution' is more or less synonymous with 'capitalism'.

*In this text, when we discuss the process of industrialization in the original British case we follow a widespread convention and refer to it as the Industrial Revolution. Where we are referring more generally to processes of industrialization, wherever they occur, then we speak of an industrial revolution or industrial revolutions.

2   Industrial revolution can refer to a particular form of *industrial organization* at the level of the unit of production, based on:

- forms of employment in which the mass of workers work for money wages, and

- the rise of the factory system bringing many workers together in a single, coordinated technical division of labour involving the widespread use of machinery. (If you need to refresh your understanding of the technical division of labour, look again at Chapter 5 in the Course Book.)

When Marx spoke of the 'capitalist mode of production' and the shift from manufacture to machinofacture this is primarily what he had in mind (see Box 2.4). As Maddison points out, Marx's interpretation of capitalist development:

> ... stressed the enormous growth of productive power represented by the transition from manufacture to machinofacture, and the importance of accelerated accumulation of fixed capital as the mainspring of economic progress.

> (Maddison, 1991, p.18)

Polanyi also devoted considerable attention to these aspects of industrial revolutions.

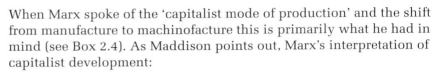

Box 2.4 Manufacture and machinofacture in Marx's Capital

In *Capital*, vol.1, Marx drew a distinction between production organized along the lines of manufacture and what he called 'machinofacture' as follows.

In the phase of manufacture, workers are brought together in factories (free wage labour working for capitalists). There is an increased degree of specialization in the performance of tasks leading to greater efficiency and increased labour productivity as a result of what Marx called the division of labour in 'detail' – this is the division of labour that Adam Smith talked about. Within the factory, the activities of specialized workers are controlled and coordinated by management, which develops in order to facilitate the control of labour by capital. Machinofacture is the phase of machinery and large-scale industry, defined by Marx thus:

'The machine, which is the starting-point of the industrial revolution, replaces the worker, who handles a single tool, by a mechanism operating with a number of similar tools and set in motion by a single motive power ... Large-scale industry therefore had to take over the machine itself ... and to produce machines by means of machines ... As machinery, the instrument of labour assumes a material mode of existence which necessitates the replacement of human forces by natural forces, and the replacement of the rule of thumb by the conscious application of modern science ... In handicrafts and manufacture, the worker makes use of a tool; in the factory, the machine makes use of him ... Machine production drives the social division of labour immeasurably further than manufacture does, because it increases the productive power of the industries it seizes upon to a much greater degree.'

(Marx, 1970, pp.497, 506, 508, 548, 572)

Both of these two conceptions of industrial revolution are important to the explanations for intensive growth identified above.

3   However, thirdly, industrial revolution may be viewed in terms of *knowledge and technology*: not only the invention and diffusion of new technical knowledge but also a condition in which such invention and diffusion becomes a permanent and systematic feature of the economy. In this respect, the critical historical break is not so much the rise of capitalist relations of production but the technology of production. Whereas agrarian economies relied on plants and animals for raw materials and on animals and humans for motive power, industrial economies augment these resources with minerals and inanimate forms of energy. Industrial economies also systematically seek to harness scientific knowledge to technical change. (Notice Marx's comment in Box 2.4 that machinofacture involves 'the replacement of the rule of thumb by the conscious application of modern science'.) Notwithstanding the watermill, windmill and sailing boat, Cipolla notes that:

... until the Industrial Revolution man continued to rely mainly on plants, animals, and other men for energy ... Hitherto the Industrial Revolution has been based essentially on the exploitation of inanimate energy derived from irreplaceable sources.

(Cipolla, 1965, pp.46, 55)

The economic historian, Eric Wrigley, argues that the fundamental change during the Industrial Revolution:

... involved the substitution of inorganic for organic inputs in most branches of industrial production; the associated revolution in the energy sources available for use in productive processes when a way was discovered of converting the energy stored in coal into useful work; and the conversion of farming from an industry engaged in coaxing the maximum net output from ecologically self-sufficient units into one in which mineral-derived inputs from outside the farm were passed though the local ecological system in such quantity as to transform not only the productivity but also the character of farming.

(Wrigley, 1987, p.10)

In short, the Industrial Revolution can be characterized as: a changing social framework; the rise of new, industrial organization; and/or as the changing role of knowledge and technology in production.

In the original British case, the social framework of the agrarian economy was commercial or capitalist sometime before intensive economic growth really gathered momentum and certainly well before the Industrial Revolution is normally understood to have begun – sometime in the second half of the eighteenth century. Moreover, in other countries, intensive economic growth and industrialization have been accomplished with quite different forms of social framework to that found in the original British case (see Sections 3 and 4 below). This reinforces the notion that transition to industrial capitalism comprises two dimensions. The English model shows a transition to commercial or capitalist forms of social organization for the economy as a whole, led by the agrarian economy. This was followed by the second dimension – a set of technological and organizational changes which revolutionized not only the rest of the economy but the agricultural sector as well (Wrigley, 1988). As we see in Section 4 below, the Soviet Union arguably provides a mirror image of this: an industrial revolution under communist forms of social organization before a later transition to capitalism.

Activity 9

How does this way of thinking about transition differ from that presented by Henry Bernstein in Chapter 11 of the Course Book?

Hint: think about Bernstein's statement about the 'acceleration' of history caused by the tendency of capitalism constantly to revolutionize technology and methods of production and to accumulate capital on an ever larger scale.

(Spend no more than 10 minutes on this)

Comment

If the view expressed above by Wrigley is correct, then we should distinguish between the transition from pre-capitalist to capitalist forms of property rights and markets, on the one hand, and the transition from an agrarian, organically based economy to an industrial economy, on the other. What Wrigley and others (see, for example, the view of Landes quoted immediately below) are getting at is the autonomous importance of industrial revolution understood as a revolution in technologies. The growth and application of knowledge, the development of revolutionary new technologies, is seen to be just as important as the discontinuity between pre-capitalist and capitalist modes of production.

It is this latter sense of technological (and to some extent organizational) change that the historian, David Landes, refers to when he defines the Industrial Revolution as:

> ... a complex of technological advances: the substitution of machines for human skills and strength, the development of inanimate sources of power (fossil fuels and the steam engine), the invention, production, and use of new materials (iron for wood, vegetable for animal matter, mineral for vegetable matter), and the introduction and spread of a new mode of production, known by contemporaries as the factory system.

The emphasis [is] on the gains in productivity and quality these changes made possible, their cumulative character, their ramification from a few leading branches into other industry and into transportation, their stimulus to creativity and innovation, and lastly the consequent gains in product and income per head.

(Landes, 1999, p.132)

Industrialization in this sense involves the mechanization of human productive activity, and the use of inanimate raw materials and sources of energy, together with large-scale factory production to reap the benefits of these means of augmenting productivity. As such, it therefore presupposes a large-scale separation of workers from the land and the diversion of a significantly increased share of the output of the economy to investment for the purposes of capital accumulation. Thus even if industrialization in this organizational and technological sense did not need to follow the commercial capitalist model that characterized British development (and it didn't), it is inconceivable that it can be accomplished without major changes to the structure of the economy, on the one hand, and the social framework of the economic system as a whole, on the other. (We will consider some of the details behind these assertions more fully in Sections 3 and 4 below.)

Understood in this sense, the Industrial Revolution was 'revolutionary', according to Joel Mokyr, 'because the technological progress it witnessed and the subsequent transformation of the economy were not ephemeral events and moved society to a *permanent* different economic trajectory' (Mokyr, 1999, p.3).*

Activity 10

To ensure that you have grasped the foregoing arguments, make sure that you can answer the following questions.

(a) What are the reasons for thinking that the advent of capitalism is decisive in moving towards intensive growth?

(b) What are the independent features of industrialization that move the economy towards intensive growth?

(You should spend about 10 minutes on this)

*Given the *irreplaceable* nature of the energy resource base of most industrialization to date (fossil fuels) and the contemporary concerns about sustainability (see Chapter 7 of the Course Book) you might want to think about Mokyr's use of the word 'permanent' in this quotation.

Comment

As we have already said, writers from very different viewpoints have noted the importance of what Bernstein calls *industrial capitalism* and what Smith referred to as *commercial society to intensive growth*. The rise of capitalism entails the rise of markets in labour, capital and raw materials and structural change in the economy that allows increasing specialization, investment and growth, driven by market competition. However, others (Wrigley and Landes above) argue that technological change towards inanimate sources of power and the integration of science and production are crucial to enabling the rises in productivity that lie behind intensive growth. For either viewpoint, the role of innovation is vital if intensive growth is to be sustained over time.

As we noted in Section 1, transition to 'industrial capitalism' really involves two different yet related transitions: *to capitalism* and *to industry*. In explaining the historical shift to intensive growth which, as we have seen, first occurred in Western Europe, different writers emphasize different sides of transition: some argue that the key shift is to capitalism; others that it is the rise of industry, relatively independently of capitalism, that is the most important aspect. We are not going to try to resolve this issue here and perhaps there is no need to choose either capitalism or industry: Marx, for example, considered both to be important.

You might like to think about the issue a little further. Would capitalism without coal, steam, iron, chemicals and the rest have produced the sustained growth in the standards of living we have documented? Conversely, can intensive growth, requiring constant innovation, be sustained over time without the driving forces of competition and profit characteristic of capitalism? These issues address some of the 'big' debates in development which you have encountered in the Course Book, such as whether the rising standard of living associated with development can be achieved without capitalism or whether industry is 'necessary' to development. We will return to these issues in Part 2 when we look at China: is it showing itself to be a case of sustained industrial transition without a transition from communism to capitalism or is it also undergoing a move to capitalism?

2.3 Summary of Section 2 and guide to the following section

Summary of Section 2

Let us try to summarize what we have established in this section. We have argued:

1 Transition involves a movement from an agrarian economy and society based on, at best, extensive growth to one based on *intensive* growth.

2 Intensive economic growth involves significant and continuous rises in per capita living standards and fundamental *structural change* in the patterns of employment and output in the economy as a whole as productivity increases and the share of total resources devoted to agriculture declines.

3 Intensive economic growth has thus far comprised:

- a change in the *social framework* of the economy as a whole as labour is 'freed' from the land and as resources are made available for capital accumulation;

- a new form of *industrial organization* based on large-scale, factory production and wage labour;

- a complex of *technological* changes centred on new *knowledge* and sources of raw materials and especially (thus far at least) inanimate forms of energy.

4 There are both 'industrial' and 'capitalist' dimensions to this transition.

Looking forward

As far as development is concerned, we saw that one of the most important consequences of the fact that the Industrial Revolution first occurred in the West was that the equality of poverty, which had characterized relations among the major agrarian civilizations, was replaced by massive inequalities of wealth and power on a worldwide scale (look again at Table 2.6 above to see this in the case of the West and China). With the significant exceptions of Japan and the Soviet Union, industrialization in the rest of the world is very largely a post-Second World War phenomenon. Nevertheless, and especially since the 1950s, a number of late-industrializing countries have increased their share of world industrial production – Japan, South Korea, Taiwan, Brazil, Mexico and China. And of the post-war industrialization, by far the most important development has been that in East Asia. This can be seen in Figure 2.3 (source: Dicken, 1998) and Table 2.7 below.

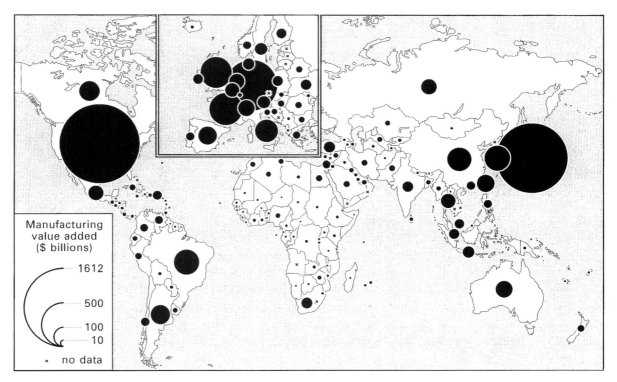

Figure 2.3 Map of world manufacturing industry, 1994.

As you can see, both South-east Asia and Latin America have increased their shares of world manufacturing output, although it is South-east Asia which has led this change. If we bear in mind the dramatic rise in importance of Japan in the spread of industrialization to East Asia as a whole, then it is easy to see how this region has dominated this most

Table 2.7 The rise of manufacturing production in South-east Asia and Latin America

	Share of world manufacturing output (%)		
	1963	1980	1994
South-east Asia[a]	0.4	5.0	8.5
South Korea	0.1	0.6	2.7
China	n.a.	2.9	2.3
Latin America[b]	2.6	4.6	4.9
Brazil	1.6	2.4	2.6

[a]South Korea, Taiwan, Hong Kong, Singapore, Malaysia, Thailand, Indonesia, Philippines, China.

[b]Brazil, Argentina, Mexico.

n.a. = data not available.

Source: adapted from Dicken, P. (1998) *Global Shift*, Paul Chapman Publishing Ltd, London, p.30, table 2.3.

recent surge in industrialization. Indeed it is no surprise that in the world 'league table' of industrial nations (in order of value-added manufacturing), South Korea was ranked sixth and China eighth by 1994 (Dicken, 1998, p.27).

In some ways this industrialization of South-east Asia is just the most recent historical example of the process of transition whereby economies have moved towards intensive growth. In this section we have investigated what this means, along with some of the underlying questions it raises. However, when we look back over the historical examples of transition, it becomes apparent that the way in which structural change happens varies from case to case. We have noted already that the British example demonstrated a move towards capitalism before the Industrial Revolution. Others, such as the Soviet Union, provide contrasting pictures and the South-east Asian cases show yet further variation.

So what can we say about these different routes to transition? First, we should note that there are some commonalities among the different historical routes. As we have noted in this section, all examples of intensive economic growth involve:

■ structural change in the economy in the movement of labour and consumption away from agriculture;

■ some means of investment of capital in production which drives productivity increases and technical specialization.

How these happen is precisely where the different transitions of Britain, Japan, the Soviet Union, South Korea and so on, vary a great deal. The next two sections are more focused on some of these dimensions – specifically the role of markets and the state in the transition process.

3 Markets and industrialization

Section 2 ended with the surge of industrialization in East Asia. This section will discuss the features of South Korea's industrialization. In particular it will focus on the role of markets in the transition to industrial capitalism. As Section 2 pointed out, all industrial transitions involve some process of structural change whereby labour is moved from agriculture to industry and investment is directed towards industrial production. These are essential if the increases in productivity and innovation in production, which underlie intensive growth, are to occur. In capitalist processes of industrialization, markets play a central role in these changes. This section begins with an outline of South Korea's transition, before taking a closer look at the role that markets play in capitalist industrialization, both in respect of the movement of labour from the land to industry and in the organization of industrial investment.

3.1 'Making capitalism': structural change in South Korea

South Korea has experienced a truly dramatic process of capitalist industrialization since 1945. In the 1950s, in the aftermath of the Korean War, some foreign observers called it an economic 'basket case', and argued that Confucian culture would get in the way of capitalist development (Janelli with Yim, 1993). Yet in 1995 South Korea joined the OECD, the 'club' of rich countries. Two anthropologists, an American and a Korean, describe the scale of the changes in people's lifetimes:

> Office workers who had spent the earliest years of their lives in rural villages without electricity later graduated from universities, drove automobiles to and from work and operated computers with ease. Affluent older managers spoke of poverty and hunger during their youth.
>
> (Janelli with Yim, 1993, p.3)

The authors go on to describe one outcome: 'the often expressed perception of South Koreans that the United States is a place where little changes'.

This pace of change is all the more remarkable if one considers that, at the beginning of the twentieth century, Korea was a poor, backward and overwhelmingly agricultural country ruled over by the Yi dynasty which had survived since the fourteenth century. From 1910 until the end of the Second World War, Korea was under Japanese colonial rule and, although the experience was a brutal one, it did weaken the power of the feudal landlord class. Korea had barely emerged from the destruction of the Second World War before it was plunged back into conflict in the Korean war of 1950–53 which resulted in the division of the country between a communist North and a US-supported, capitalist South. It was in emerging from this turbulent period that South Korea's transition to industrial capitalism took hold.

Rapid industrialization in South Korea involved precisely the processes that we have identified already: a huge shift of people from working the land into offices and factories, and the rise of industrial firms. Thus, between 1960 and 1980, the percentage of South Koreans making their living as farmers fell from 72% to 28%, a dramatic rate of out-migration (Lie, 1998, p.111). A South Korean political economist, Lie (1998, p.16) described his own family's 'chain migration' to Seoul, as the income gap grew between urban and rural areas: his paternal grandparents first sent their sons to school in Seoul, then married their daughters to men who found jobs in Seoul, and finally moved to join their children. People who had previously been tied to the land and subservient to landowners now had to work for a wage in urban industrial areas.

A key development in this creation of a labour market was the land reform process set in train during the Korean War. The communist North had already begun distributing rights to land to peasants and as its forces moved south the government in Seoul, fearing that communist policy would be popular among the rural poor, also redistributed land and set an upper limit on landholding of 7.5 acres (3.0 ha). This meant land could no longer serve as the basis for great wealth. The effects, described by Lie (1998) were to:

- reduce rural poverty, and
- destroy both the landlord class and the link between land and social status.

He quotes his maternal grandmother: 'Land is meaningless; you can't carry it around with you.' The rural poor who were more able and inclined to move from the land formed the basis of the emerging industrial labour force.

Forced to look elsewhere for avenues to protect and increase their wealth, the élite also turned to the industrial sector to invest its resources. New Korean-owned companies were the main source of employment for the new urban workers. South Korean industrialization was notable for its low reliance on foreign multinational companies investing in Korea from outside. Instead, very large South Korean owned industrial groups, called *chaebol*, were created by a process of diversification of production into a wide range of sectors. These *chaebol* borrowed investment funds from abroad, while keeping the ownership of equity – that is, the shares in the company – predominantly in local hands (Amsden, 1989). They also benefited from US aid in the early years after the war as well as the support of the Korean state. They thus represented the rise to prominence of a new kind of capitalist, industrial company in Korea. The last forty years of the twentieth century therefore saw the creation of a South Korean bourgeoisie: a social class of owners and senior managers of a burgeoning private industrial sector (Amsden, 1989).

Activity 11

We defined transition in Section 1 as involving structural change in society as a whole, brought about by the development of industrail capitalism; South Korea has undergone an extraordinarily rapid transition to industrial capitalism. Read carefully the definition of *structure* in Section 1.2. On the basis of the above description of South Korea's industrialization, make a list of several major changes in social and economic structure associated with transition to capitalist industrial society.

(Spend about 10 minutes on this)

Comment

'Structural change' in the transition to industrial capitalist society in South Korea, described above, included:

- a shift from agrarian working relationships to industrial wage labour;
- a shift in the nature of the social and economic élite, from landholding to industrial ownership and management;
- migration from rural to urban areas;
- a change in the pattern of production and consumption towards industrial goods.

South Korea's transition also involved the creation of a state deeply involved with the industrial élite in the industrialization process. Under authoritarian military control from 1961, the state was active in controlling the new labour force and encouraging industrial investment. We return to the role of the state below. However, at the same time, markets in labour and capital increased in importance in the economy and society. A central dimension of the transition to industrial capitalism is indeed the extension of the role of markets in society and here we take a closer look at this. We will first consider what markets are, before analysing their role in respect of labour and capital.

3.2 Markets and structural change

Markets in 'the great transformation': the arguments of Karl Polanyi

This subsection develops in a bit more detail some concepts needed to analyse the 'thunderous' structural change that transition entails. Capitalist industrialization in the nineteenth and early twentieth centuries was experienced as just as dramatic and painful a transition as the more recent South Korean experience: hence the description of that transition by Karl Polanyi (Course Book, Chapter 1) as 'the great transformation'. You have met Polanyi's arguments at various points in the Course Book; we are going to build on them here to analyse transition, so let us start by reviewing them.

But first, who was Karl Polanyi? (See Figure 3.1.)

He was born in the 1880s, in the Vienna of the Austro–Hungarian Empire, and lived through two world wars and into the 1960s. He was

Figure 3.1 Karl Polanyi

successively an army officer, a university teacher and a financial journalist in Vienna. He fled central Europe in 1934 to escape Fascist persecution, becoming a British citizen and living in Britain and the US during the 1939–45 war. He was a writer and academic. He wrote his most famous book *The Great Transformation*, during that war, debating its arguments, as he notes in his preface, with his students at Workers' Education Association classes in London and Kent in 1939 and 1940. The book was published in 1944, before the end of the war.

This gives his book a particular standpoint. Like many earlier writers during the Industrial Revolution, and many in developing countries today, he was writing from within an experience of a world that seemed to have gone mad. Social relationships he had grown up with had disintegrated around him under the weight of economic depression, Fascist government, exile and war. In this, his standpoint resembles that of many people today: Tim Allen's chapter 'A World at War' in the Course Book made clear the scale of contemporary worldwide experience of war and associated social and economic disintegration and dislocation. Polanyi sought, as Tim Allen seeks in that chapter, for roots of these conflicts in politics and economics. And in his explanations, Polanyi focused on the role of *markets*.

Activity 12

Using the index, go through the Course Book and make a list of some of Polanyi's key ideas as described by the authors of the various chapters that draw upon his work, looking in particular for his arguments about markets.

(Spend about 15 minutes on this)

Comment

Your answer may have included:

- Economic improvement may come at the price of social dislocation (p.3).
- A 'great transformation' into industrial capitalism and a market society created a tendency to 'self destruction' of that society (p.4). This self destruction is the result, not of markets as such, but the development of 'self-regulating markets' not only in commodities to be consumed, but also in land and labour power and productive organization (pp.25–26, 39).
- Capitalism is characterized by a struggle between those political forces promoting this extension of 'commoditization' into land, labour and organization, and those forces opposed (pp.35–36, 40).
- The 'great transformation' of the economy began (in Britain) in the late eighteenth century (p.241). Before this time, land and labour were 'embedded' in social relations, institutions, beliefs and values. As a result, people sought not individual gain but to safeguard social standing (pp.263, 326–327). Self-regulating markets – those that respond unhindered to supply and demand – separate out economic concerns from social relations. The economy is 'disembedded', individual gain becomes the motive of members of society, and social relationships become subordinated to the market. Industrialization critically requires this disembedding (p.327).

■ People, labour and money are 'fictitious' commodities, and the state in the nineteenth century sought to protect them from the worst effects of their entry into markets during industrialization. Such protection is essential in industrial society (pp.327–328).

Taken together, these form a striking, contentious, and difficult set of ideas. One of the key points is that industrialization involves a tearing up of the existing 'social fabric' of a society – the destruction of traditional social relations and ties – and their replacement with 'disembedded' market relations where everything can become a commodity to be bought and sold. Polanyi thought such a move was dangerous, leading to social breakdown unless countermeasures were taken limiting the scope of the market (what he terms 'protection'). The discussion in the Course Book thus locates Polanyi in a number of bigger intellectual and political contexts: structuralism; economic liberalism and its contestants in two centuries; Marxism and its opponents. What we hope to do here is to develop and build upon Polanyi's key theme: *that the way markets work crucially shapes transition to industrial capitalism.*

Making markets

A good deal of Polanyi's argument, as just described, revolves around two crucial questions about markets:

What is bought and sold on markets (or, what is '*commodified*'), and with what consequences for society?

Are markets '*self-regulating*' and what are the consequences of that?

First, what is market exchange?

Activity 13

Below are some examples of *exchange*: that is, situations where something is given in return for something else. Which of these do you think are examples of *market exchange*? Give reasons for your answers.

(Spend about 20 minutes on this)

1   A cattle herder sells milk and uses the money to buy grain and salt.
2   The cattle herder pastures cattle on a farmer's cleared field and receives grain in return for manure and milk.
3   The cattle herder sells emaciated cattle at very low prices in famine times.
4   A worker goes to work in a car factory and is paid at the end of the week.
5   A Prime Minister receives his monthly salary from the state whose government he leads.
6   Someone with malaria pays a private-sector doctor for treatment.
7   Someone with malaria pays a fee to a government hospital for treatment.
8   A householder buys electricity from a private company; there is no alternative supplier and the government controls prices.
9   Someone buys milk in a corner shop.
10 Someone buys yoghurt from neighbours who make it themselves.

Comment

We hope that if you thought about this carefully, you may have concluded that the answer depends on a careful definition of 'market'. For example, you might have decided that only 2 is not a market exchange, on the grounds that it is the only one that does not involve money. That would define a market by the use of money. On the other hand, you might have had doubts about 5 and 7 – and perhaps even 4 since the ownership of the car factory is not stated. If we pay the government, or the government pays us, is this a market exchange, or is a 'market' defined by privately owned providers? One possible reply is that 6 and 7 are both market exchanges if the ill person can choose private or public, but that 4 and 7 might not be market exchanges if the government owned all the car factories and hospitals and set the prices and wages. In which case what about 8? Perhaps this is not a market exchange either, if markets are defined by choice for the purchaser.

You might furthermore have had doubts about 3, 5 and 10 because each of these seems to have something odd about the buyer–seller relationship and the price-setting process. Does the politician's involvement in setting his or her own salary undermine the claim that this is a 'market' exchange of work for money? Does the fact that you know your neighbours well mean that their yoghurt has aspects of a gift: perhaps they do not ask a 'market price'? And in 3, the herder is forced into the market to trade on unfavourable terms. Is forced trade a market exchange?

There is no single accepted definition of a market, but these examples illustrate a number of the relevant issues. Markets generally operate through some kind of money, though this is not always in the familiar forms – shells once acted as money in West Africa and cigarettes can be money in prison camps. Markets also require some competition among suppliers and choice by buyers. Markets monopolized by one seller, whether public or private, are scarcely markets at all. In most markets competition among suppliers is rooted in private ownership: individuals and private firms own the goods they sell and retain the proceeds. However, market competition can also occur between publicly and co-operatively owned firms. Markets imply some price setting mechanism involving interaction between suppliers and purchasers, though this may not be highly competitive. And there are some definitional issues around repetition of exchange and motivations: markets may not be impersonal – you may know your corner shopkeeper well – but a casual purchase of your neighbour's home product may be more about friendship than shopping. Finally, there is an ethical issue. Most people would define forced sale as still a market sale, but the strong cultural associations between markets and freedom make this an uneasy definition.

Markets long pre-date industrialization, but capitalist industrialization entails a huge rise in the number and complexity of markets for two reasons.

1   The production of goods for sale in a market is one of the defining features of capitalism and any transition to industrial capitalism therefore involves a central and expanding role for markets in shaping production and consumption.

2   Markets are important because industrialization typically involves a huge rise in the number and complexity of goods and services that are produced, bought and sold.

Markets enable this to happen. In Section 4 you will see some of the difficulties encountered in the Soviet attempt to suppress key markets and replace them by administrative co-ordination of industrial activity.

However, there remains a question of how markets come about in a process of transition: how are markets 'made'? Here the real controversy gets under way, and the way we address this shapes the rest of this section. There are two distinct views that persist through many generations of thinkers and policy makers. One view is that markets tend to emerge naturally where they are free to do so, when barriers, which prevent or limit exchange or which prevent some things from being commodified, disappear. This is the framework of thought behind the concept of 'liberalization' of markets. The second view is that markets are institutions – established social practices and activities – that have to be consciously constructed, a political and economic process that has frequently involved the use of force. Polanyi was a powerful advocate of the second view. We can illustrate these two views from the debate about South Korean, and more broadly East Asian, industrialization.

Markets as natural processes: incentives and liberalization

Much of economic analysis consists in exploring the *incentives* offered by particular institutional processes – such as market trading, or taxation, or contracts for wage labour – for the behaviour of individual participants. The basic model or conception of a market in economic analysis is of a process of trading among individuals or firms, where participants' behaviour responds to changes in price. Price changes create incentives for changes in quantities bought and sold, for example rising prices:

- provide incentives to consumers to seek alternative goods to satisfy consumption needs;
- provide incentives to producers to seek alternative inputs for production;
- may encourage producers of the goods that are rising in price to produce more.

The causes of price changes are sought in people's changing preferences for goods, and in changes in costs of production of firms and in their competitive strategies. In this economic modelling of markets, prices convey *information* about costs and preferences, so that, for example, competing suppliers have incentives to reduce costs of production and to respond effectively to consumer demand. The existence of *competition* is thus crucial to these economic models of markets.

This approach to analysing markets has numerous limitations, but let us first pause on its strengths. Markets do create strong incentives to change behaviour, and firms and individuals do respond. If those incentives are misleading, huge economic costs can ensue: the financial and economic crisis in East Asia in 1997, discussed later in this section, can be traced in part to just such misleading economic signals. Conversely, if the incentives are the right ones, they can help to drive industrial growth. The World Bank has attributed much – not all – of the success of East Asian, including South Korean, industrialization to 'market friendly' policies:

> How have the East Asian economies succeeded in using resources efficiently? ... Price distortions, while present, were limited and markets were allowed to work. HPAE [High-Performing Asian Economies] ... opened up much of the modern economy to international competition and introduced world prices as performance standards, not only for exports but also for the intermediate and capital goods used in export production.
>
> (World Bank, 1993, p.260)

You should note that in this quotation, by the 'modern economy' the World Bank means the large scale industrial sector.

Some aspects of the argument in this passage are well supported by evidence. Analysts of East Asian industrial success from Japanese industrialization onwards generally acknowledge the importance of competition in manufactured export markets in driving local firms into technological and industrial change. South Korea kept its exchange rate low by devaluing the currency regularly; the effect was to help to make exports price-competitive on international markets. Exporters paid no tariffs (taxes) on imports (World Bank, 1993). Furthermore, competition within the domestic consumer market was sharp, despite the small number of large firms supplying domestic markets, focusing on a tussle for market share in a growing market (Amsden and Singh, 1994).

Markets as created social institutions

More controversial in the World Bank's view just quoted was the idea that 'markets were allowed to work'. Alice Amsden, an industrial economist who has studied East Asian economic development over many years, argues that in contrast, South Korean and other East Asian growth was 'market augmenting': markets were consciously constructed and shaped. This perspective is closer to Polanyi's approach: instead of studying markets' operation as trading interaction among individuals, the focus is on *market making*: the actions of governments, the social networks and power relations, and the institutional processes that shape behaviour in markets. Examples of such market making include establishing the legal and regulatory structure of markets; the enforcement – or lack of enforcement – of private ownership of property; the development of market culture, including the expectations of contracting parties and the institutional organization of firms, labour and consumers; and the use of state funding to change participants' incentives.

Critics of the World Bank's arguments on East Asian industrialization argue that these processes of 'governing the market' (Wade, 1990) are crucial to understanding how industrial growth occurred. Far from success arising from 'getting the prices right' (a free market catch-phrase of the 1980s):

> Government policies deliberately got some prices 'wrong', so as to change the signals to which decentralized market agents responded, and also used non-price means to alter the behaviour of market agents.
>
> (Wade, 1990, p.29)

Wade goes on to argue that the Taiwanese state 'steered' resource allocation 'in line with the long-term national interest'. Amsden's (1989) study of South Korean industrialization broadly takes this line. She too argues that the South Korean government deliberately got prices 'wrong', in the sense of shifting price signals away from those generated by current market processes, in the interests of long-term industrialization. Her examples include extensive subsidies to successful exporters, but *only* for the successful: she recounts a number of examples of 'the government's cold-bloodedness towards poorly managed firms in distress' (Amsden, 1989, p.15). The price advantages offered to successful international exporters included the ability to borrow funds abroad at low cost. Profits allocated to Research and Development could be protected from taxes. Furthermore Korean firms' sales to their domestic market were protected by tariffs on imports.

Note that Amsden and Wade are *not* arguing that market participants (or 'agents') do not respond to incentives. Rather they are arguing that a view that characterizes markets solely by analysing observed incentive structures is so incomplete as to be wrong: it misses the ways in which markets – and their incentives structures – are 'made'.

Activity 14

In order to check your own understanding of this discussion, note down the distinction between the two views of markets (as emerging naturally and as created social institutions) and the different interpretations of East Asian transition that they lead to.

(If you have difficulty doing this, take another look at this section)

Different ideas about markets have thus led to very different interpretations of East Asia's industrialization. We established earlier (Section 2) that transition to industrial capitalism involves (a) the movement of labour away from agriculture to industry and (b) industrial investment. We now turn to tracing the alternative views of markets through the creation of a wage labour market and the creation of capital or finance markets, together with the linked issue of private property, which enable industrial investment. We show that our alternative conceptions of markets lead to rather different understandings of what happened in South Korea.

3.3 Trading labour

The making of 'free' labour

The movement of labour out of agriculture and small scale production of goods and services into larger scale manufacturing, mining and service production has been described as the creation of a 'free' labour force: free, that is, from ties to the land. Throughout history, this process has been marked by high levels of violence and misery. It has seen huge changes in the culture and social organization of people's lives, as they migrated to mines and cities, adapted to life in factories or struggled to find wage employment, and organized themselves to try to challenge the worst of the circumstances they faced.

This huge change has happened during industrialization in both capitalist and planned economies. However, the extent to which this enormous upheaval creates a *market* for people's labour varies hugely, as do the terms on which labour is sold. In order to see what Polanyi meant by 'disembedding' of labour in industrialization, and to develop our own views on his arguments, we need to look more carefully at this problematic notion of a labour market.

An industrial work force may be created in two ways: by attracting people into industry and/or by forcing them off the land. In many cases a combination of both occurs. Polanyi documented two major forces creating the industrial working class in England:

- the *agricultural revolution*, which enclosed common land and created a large class of landless labourers (and which often involved violent removal of people from land they had traditionally had rights to), and

- the *Poor Law Reforms* of the 1830s that abolished 'outdoor relief' (a form of what we would now call social assistance), and which therefore presented the now landless labourers with a choice between industrial wage labour or hunger.

Box 3.1 Poor Law Reforms

In Britain in the late eighteenth century and early nineteenth century, the 'old poor law' (often referred to as the 'Speenhamland system') gave social assistance to the landless poor but only if they remained in their 'home' parish. However, given the falling demand for labour in agricultural areas, it did nothing to solve the problem of rural poverty in the long term and was a disincentive for labour to move to the newly emerging industrial centres. Eventually, after a long campaign waged partly by the leaders of the emerging industrial bourgeoisie, the system was reformed, breaking the ties to the parish and introducing the hated workhouse as the main means by which social assistance was granted and forcing people to move to the towns to find work. This, together with the explosion of demand for industrial labour in the 1830s and 1840s, helped to create a massive shift in labour away from traditional rural areas and to the new cities and towns of industrial Britain.

The experience of the early stages of industrialization for those who took up work in factories, mines and sweatshops – which may be the only stages of industrialization ever reached in many countries – has generally been bad. Karl Marx's analysis of capitalism was deeply influenced by the dreadful conditions of life in early nineteenth-century industrial cities. Across the world and a century later, South Korean early industrialization was marked by low wages, casualized employment, and very poor working conditions – including very long working hours. Women's wages and conditions were particularly dreadful, and labour-intensive exports in the 1970s depended heavily on women workers. Urban poverty was widespread, and the military regime engaged in violent repression of labour organization and student protest (Amsden, 1989; Lie, 1998).

Polanyi argued, with Marx before him and many socialist, social democratic and trade union commentators after him, that in early capitalist industrialization the mix of labour repression, lack of social assistance, and more people seeking jobs than are able to find them, tends to drive down wages below subsistence levels. The market incentives in these circumstances are thus disastrous for those seeking employment. Marx quoted, in *Capital*, a British member of parliament who argued, in 1863, that the cotton textile mills, existing for ninety years or three generations, had in that time 'destroyed nine generations of factory operatives'. In capitalist countries where industrialization eventually generates higher incomes – and South Korea in the mid-1990s joined the OECD, the 'club of the rich' – some institutional processes have to intervene to break this disastrous spiral. These will generally involve government regulation or intervention.

Regulation, incentives and real wages

What kinds of intervention can limit downward pressure on wages? Typically, this has required government regulation of the terms for hiring labour and can take the form of regulation of minimum labour conditions, minimum working days, minimum wages, and legalization of union organizing and bargaining. Such regulation – often furiously resisted by employers and many in government – has frequently emerged from the often violent interaction of labour organizations and government and employers. It is this kind of struggle which Polanyi identified when he talked of a tension between efforts to commodify labour and efforts to protect society against the destructive results of this extension of the market. Regulation has nevertheless helped to generate an upward spiral of a more educated, higher paid workforce operating more productively. One of the most prescient chapters in *Capital*, Volume 1, is Marx's analysis, in just these terms, of the struggle to restrict the length of the working day.

Another way in which governments can influence the terms of the wage bargain, and put a floor under real wages, is by directly influencing the returns to alternatives to wage labour, or by investing directly in raising labour productivity. Both interventions change the incentives facing firms and workers. In South Korea, land reform raised rural incomes and thereby put a floor under the wages that male industrial workers would accept. Furthermore, the government invested heavily in education, developing from a high level of literacy inherited from the period of Japanese colonialism (Amsden, 1989). In the 1960s, Korea became an exporter of educated labour, a situation that changed as industrialization accelerated in the 1970s. Finally, government pressure to export created incentives for the *chaebol* to train and retain the skilled labour needed to achieve high productivity levels, pushing up wages for blue collar workers who remained with a firm once trained. From a base of very low wages by international standards in the 1950s, South Korea saw real wages for men in manufacturing rise fast in later decades of industrialization. Women workers, however, were largely left out of this wage-productivity spiral, and in the early 1980s South Korean women's hourly wage in manufacturing was less than half that of men (Amsden, 1989).

The World Bank's analysis of South Korean labour market development (World Bank, 1993) also traces this pattern of low wages followed by rising wages and productivity, but the emphasis in its explanation differs from that of the more political economists cited above. The World Bank focuses on the extent to which the South Korean Government stayed *out* of direct labour market regulation. It points to its:

- willingness to see wages remain low in early industrialization,
- low spending on social security (forcing people to work for low wages), and
- repression of labour organization

as factors in creating wage 'flexibility' until labour shortages emerged, so that industrial jobs paid only a relatively small premium over agricultural wages. The World Bank (1993, p.272) describes this as wages set at 'market clearing' rates, and notes that East Asian governments did *not* expand public sector employment to reduce unemployment. Once labour shortages appeared, employers had an incentive to move to more skill-intensive production methods, and hence to raise wages to encourage workers to invest in education and training. The emphasis here is on:

- the ability of markets to provide information, or signals, and to provide incentives for shifts in behaviour, and
- the role of government in enforcing the conditions for a competitive labour market.

Activity 15

Try answering these questions without going back to the text. If you have difficulty with this, re-read Section 3.3.

(a) What are the two mechanisms by which labour can be moved from the land into industrial production during transition?

(b) List the actions of government that can influence the terms on which labour is exchanged in the market.

(c) Briefly contrast the government interventions emphasized by the World Bank as important for enforcing a competitive labour market with those interventions most likely to be demanded by organized labour.

(Spend about 15 minutes on this)

Comment

You will have noted that labour can be moved from the land to industry through *incentives* or through *force*. Historically, there have been combinations of both. The British case showed the importance of incentives (the reform of the poor law) but this took place against a backdrop where the (often violent) removal of people's rights to land had already taken place. As you will see in Section 4, the Soviet Union is an example where extreme violence was used to remove labour from the land. And in South Korea the violent disruption of Japanese colonialism and two wars weakened traditional ties and increased the incentives to move into industry.

Once this movement occurs, as we noted, conditions are often very harsh. But struggle between labour on the one hand and the state and employers on the other helps to shape various forms of intervention in industry which can modify the conditions under which labour is employed. The pattern of intervention will vary from place to place – in South Korea it was evident in land reform, investment in education, the use of incentives to companies to export as well as repression of labour organizations. Minimum wages, regulation of the length of the working day and health and safety legislation also affect the terms on which labour is exchanged.

The World Bank's analysis of South Korea emphasized government actions that forced people into the labour market at low wages and prevented labour organizing: that is, actions that enforced a competitive low-wage labour market until the moment when employers sought to pay more to attract skilled workers. Labour organizations, by contrast, tend to seek protective regulation to defend their members from very low pay and poor working conditions.

There is thus widespread agreement that some interventions – including force, legislation and persuasion – are involved in the making of labour markets. But while one perspective – seeing markets as actively 'made' – tends to emphasize detailed intervention in the terms of labour hiring, the other perspective identifies the role of intervention in forcing markets to emerge by removing impediments to competition. A similar tension runs through analysis of the other key processes of transition involving the ownership, investment and trading of capital.

3.4 Owning, investing and trading capital

The structural change underpinning transition to industrial capitalism also involves the rise of industrial investment (Section 2). The role of investment in industrial production is vital to the increases in productivity that are central to intensive growth, and private investment in production of goods and services for sale in a market is a defining feature of capitalism. For capital to be traded on a market it first has to be owned and so we begin by looking at the notion of private property, then at the emergence of large, privately owned industrial organizations, and finally at the emergence of financial markets.

Property rights and privatization

The rise of industrial capitalism in Britain, South Korea and elsewhere required the emergence of institutions to support the assembly of large-scale investment funds. These were an essential part of the emergence of the factory system and the concentration of labour into large industrial production units. However, the way in which such investment is organized varied historically. In Britain, the emergence of an agrarian capitalism before industrialization had already played an important part in concentrating private ownership of wealth in the hands of a rich élite. In the early years of the Industrial Revolution the relatively low level of technological development and limited size of factory meant that wealthy individuals could invest their own money in their own industrial enterprises. However, as industrial production developed, this individual owning and controlling of production became less and less feasible as the scale and complexity of production escalated and some means of organizing finance from many different investors became necessary. This was particularly true of later industrializing countries such as Germany, Japan and South Korea.

For anyone to have the confidence to invest in a particular industrial enterprise certain safeguards or institutional frameworks are needed. Key examples of these are the legal framework for the **limited liability company** and the development of the **stock market**. An investor in a limited liability company is liable – should the company go bankrupt – only for the funds invested; the shares owned by such individuals, known as the 'equity' of the company, can be traded on stock markets, so the investing individual can retrieve his or her capital, though perhaps at a loss. These two institutions together created the framework for the public limited companies ('plcs') or (in the US) corporations that dominate large scale industrial activity today.

> **Limited liability company:** An investor in a public limited company is liable, should it go bankrupt, only for the amount he or she has invested. The company's creditors cannot have access to the individual's personal wealth or to investments in other companies.

Stock market: Company shares are traded on stock markets. The London (UK) and Wall Street (US) stock exchanges are among the most well known.

Underpinning these and other institutional frameworks is the institution of private property itself.

Janos Kornai[*] argues that *property rights*, and specifically 'the dominant position of private property' is thus the crucial distinctive feature of the capitalist system, necessarily associated with political power that is 'friendly to private property' though not necessarily democratic (Kornai, 2000, p.29). Every reform programme in Eastern Europe and the ex-Soviet countries after 1990 has had privatization of state companies as a key policy (but not always successfully). In parallel fashion, some explanations of East Asia's success in capitalist industrialization include the benefit of relatively secure property rights and effective enforceability of contract, in contrast to lesser security of property rights elsewhere. This is an argument that we shall question, for the specific case of China, in Part 2 of this Theme, so we should pause here and examine the concept of 'property rights' more closely. This concept is an analytical tool you will use again later in the Theme.

[*]Janos Kornai is an eminent Hungarian economist and influential theorist of the economics of 'existing socialism' in Eastern Europe before 1990.

Economists give the concept of property rights a rather different meaning than common parlance. They divide up property rights into a bundle of different attributes defined by what a person or firm can do with something in which he or she has some ownership. These include:

- the right to use something (for example to farm land);
- the right to alienate it (to give it away, to sell or otherwise dispose of it);
- the right to transform it (for example to use it as an input to a production process);
- the right to appropriate the product (for example to eat or sell farm produce).

This framework of thought implies that property rights are never complete: rather, that we can analyse a spectrum of rights. We have more or less power to use and dispose of things we have, depending, for example, on regulations concerning waste disposal or the organization of productive processes, or planning regulations on land. Private ownership is not something that we have or do not have; it is something we have more or less strongly and in different dimensions. Furthermore, this framework of thought emphasizes relationships: property rights are established in relation to the rights of others and the rule of law and the state. Finally, property rights establish incentives. The stronger are rights of disposal, for example, the more willing people may be to invest; the stronger are rights to the product, the more incentive there may be to increase productive efficiency. It is this last point that is emphasized in the literature on transition. Privatization in Britain and other European countries was expected to improve incentives for efficient use of labour and investment capital by private owners; similar arguments are made concerning the benefits of privatizing state firms in ex-socialist economies. The emergence of private property rights in transitions from pre-industrial societies has been a vital component of the rise of industrial investment.

Large firms and private industrialists

How then is private industrial property created in the transition to industrial capitalism? South Korean history offers one example of the inter-relationships between market incentives and government action in the creation of both large capitalist firms and a capitalist class in rapid industrialization. Korean industrial growth occurred through the creation, expansion and diversification of the privately owned industrial groups called *chaebol*. The capital that was invested in these companies in the early years came from several sources, including surplus funds that could no longer (after land reform) be invested in agriculture, and windfall gains to the élite from post-war US aid funds. Later, as industrialization accelerated, government subsidy for exporters (including cheap credit from government-owned banks) and overseas borrowing became important sources of funds. The government closely regulated the numbers of firms entering particular sectors, and the South Korean industrial sector became extraordinarily concentrated: in 1974 sales by the top 10 *chaebol* represented 15% of GDP; by 1984, the figure was 67% by which time just three *chaebol* produced over a third of GDP (Amsden, 1989, p.116).

These huge industrial groups were in private – indeed family – hands. However, they were deeply involved with, and restricted by, government action. Their profitability was underpinned by state subsidy, and they were periodically rescued by government in recessions. However, their access to credit from nationalized banks was conditional on meeting export performance targets, and on continuing to diversify and grow: hence the continuing incentive to compete for markets. And their access to overseas credit was the result of their undoubted commercial success. The *chaebol* in the 1970s and 1980s were *both* highly successful private enterprises – and enterprises whose activity was strongly shaped by government decisions on the provision of industrial licences, credit and subsidy.

As the *chaebol* have diversified, they have created new markets along with new products: this is what Amsden meant by 'market augmenting' industrialization. Thus the transition to industrial capitalism is not so much a process of 'privatization' as of the creation of capitalist firms and private markets where they did not exist before. Amsden quotes the chairman of a *chaebol*, the Lucky Goldstar group, in the mid-1980s, when it has a turnover of over US$9bn:

My father and I started a cosmetic cream factory in the late 1940s. At the time, no company could supply us with plastic caps of adequate quality for cream jars, so we had to start a plastics business. Plastic caps alone were not sufficient to run the plastic-moulding plant, so we added combs, tooth brushes and soap boxes. This plastic business also led us to manufacture electrical and electronic products and telecommunications equipment. The plastics business also took us into oil refining, which needed a tanker-shipping company. The oil refining company alone was paying an insurance premium amounting to more than half the total revenue of the then largest insurance company in Korea. Thus an insurance company was started...

(Harvard Business School, 1985, quoted in Amsden, 1989, p.126)

Behind this 'step by step evolution' is a key feature of South Korean industrialization: the low level of direct investment by foreign companies. Market gaps, as they opened up in the growing economy, were filled by local diversification by export-oriented local companies.

Activity 16

Make some notes on the ways in which the South Korean Government shaped the structure of industrial firms. Contrast this with at least one way in which the firms made their own markets.

(Spend about 10 minutes on this)

Comment

The Government created incentives for growth through subsidies and access to credit based on performance. It regulated the number of firms. The *chaebol* actively developed export markets overseas and sought out overseas credit. Both firms and governments shape industrial markets.

However, for any of these incentives to be effective some means of moving resources from one area of investment to another is necessary. This is where financial markets come in.

Financial markets

By 'financial markets', economists and journalists mean the borrowing and lending of money, and trade in many varieties of financial assets. Financial assets are best defined by example: they include shareholdings in private companies, company and government bonds (a tradable loan certificate), and holdings of tradable foreign currencies. These financial markets are crucial to the day-to-day operation of industrial capitalism: companies and governments borrow the funds that allow their daily operations; companies are valued by investors on these markets; individuals deposit their savings against a rainy – or inflationary – day.

Polanyi argued that 'self-regulating' – or unregulated – markets in money were particularly problematic, and that it was with good reason that governments typically imposed tight regulation. Those anxieties sound very contemporary. There are few people – though there *are* a few – who argue for completely deregulated financial markets, but most economic analysis emphasizes the importance of effective government regulation, for example of bank lending behaviour, to try to prevent financial crashes. However, within this consensus, economists and historians debate the role of fairly free or managed markets in twentieth-century capitalist industrialization, for example in East Asia.

There is a strong strand of argument in the economic literature for financial liberalization as a development policy. The argument goes that reducing state control over banking, interest rates and exchange rates has a number of beneficial effects on industrialization. Interest rates tend to rise, providing an incentive for the population to save, allowing high rates of investment. Efficiency of investment is increased because funds can flow to the most profitable uses, and competition for funds creates an incentive for efficiency. Firms can borrow on international financial markets, and foreign investment brings access to new resources including technology and know-how. The 'market-friendly' interpretation of East Asian success in industrialization tends to focus on positive real interest rates and high savings rates.

The alternative, 'governed market' view of financial markets in East Asian industrialization emphasizes the positive aspects of government involvement for development, such as cheap loans from South Korean nationalized banks to exporters and to favoured sectors such as automobiles, and the ability to 'lead' market development rather than follow it.

In South Korea, the government nationalized the banks in 1961, at the beginning of the era of military government. Liberalization – the gradual privatization of the commercial banks – began only in the 1980s. Some commercial banks moved into the control of the *chaebol*. Domestic credit was thus closely shaped by government and later industrial group decisions. The *chaebol* also borrowed on the international financial markets. In the international debt crisis of the early 1980s, South Korea emerged as one of the biggest international debtors; however, its growth rate was so rapid that it was never in real danger of international default. It was not until 1997 that the country's vulnerability to international financial markets turned into a crisis when, following economic and financial problems in Japan, much of East Asia (except China) faced the collapse of its financial institutions, the crisis threatening to take many industrial firms with it.

Analysis of the causes of the crisis draw on these two perspectives on financial markets. Those critical of liberalization emphasize the greater build-up of private debt in the 1990s, and point to failures of regulation. In 1996, the South Korean economy's growth slowed, and highly indebted firms' profitabilities fell sharply. In early 1997 the fourteenth largest *chaebol* declared bankruptcy, beginning a chain of business failures. Those in favour of financial liberalization point rather to the continuing close relationship between government, banks and industrial firms as the root of the problem of firms' debts. In November 1997, South Korea had finally to seek international financial support to avoid defaulting on external debt. The result was a severe economic recession in South Korea in 1998, and the first experience of widespread unemployment for decades. In 1999, however, growth restarted, and South Korea was in 2000 – and startlingly – growing again at about 8% a year.

Whatever the interpretation of the 1990s crisis, we can see how the two views of markets – as naturally emerging and as socially created – also inform our understanding of how financial markets come about and operate.

3.5 Industrialization, market creation and the role of the state

Summary of Section 3

In Section 2 we saw how the structural changes involved in the transition to industrial capitalism enabled societies to move towards intensive economic growth and rising standards of living. In Section 3 we have gone further into the notion of structural change by looking at how the transition to industrial capitalism entails, in particular, the rise of markets as a means for organizing the movement of labour and investment capital into industrial production. However, throughout this section we have also questioned how far we can see markets as things that simply emerge wherever they are allowed to. Indeed we have shown through the case of South Korea how markets rely on 'non-market' activity to come into being. Furthermore, the way that markets operate on a day-to-day basis is crucially shaped by the non-market actions of a variety of groups and actors. None is more important than the state.

Activity 17

Think back over the material covered in Section 3 and consider in what ways the state has had an impact on the structural changes evident in South Korea's transition in terms of:

(a) the creation of a wage labour force by separation of labour from the land;

(b) the creation of new forms of private property;

(c) the accumulation of wealth and investment in large industrial organizations.

(Spend 15–20 minutes on this)

Comment

As you will probably have noted, in each of these areas the state has been important. It was the government – albeit under Japanese colonial control (which lasted from 1910 until 1945) – which began the process of weakening the control of the landlord class in Korea and the movement of labour into the cities to the new industrial production centres. And it was the government promotion of land reform in the early 1950s which sealed the fate of the traditional ties between labour and the land in rural areas. Furthermore, in the immediate aftermath of the war and the liberation from Japanese rule, the government closely regulated the newly emerging industrial working class through repression of independent organization. Perhaps more obviously, the government played a central role in the organization of investment into the *chaebol* which were at the centre of Korea's rapid industrialization. And the government closely regulated the financial markets which have been so important in South Korea's industrialization.

So, while the creation of markets is indeed a central part of transition, any account of transition must also deal with the role of the state in the processes of transition. Section 4 takes up this issue.

4 The state and industrialization

If the case of South Korea suggests the importance of assessing the role of states in addition to markets, the necessity of this task is demonstrated further if we look at other cases of industrialization such as that of the Soviet Union. In Section 4.1 we will explore further the idea that states are powerful and important actors in transitions by looking at a case where for many years the state itself undertook many of the key structural changes which we have already identified. However, this role raises questions about how the state is able to act so decisively. To answer this demands that we have some notion of what we mean by 'the state' in the first place, and how transitions raise issues not just about the role of the state in promoting changes in the rest of society but also how the relationship between the state and society is itself transformed. This will be dealt with in Section 4.2.

4.1 What happens when the state itself undertakes transition?

This subsection focuses on those activities of the state that promote some of the structural transformations we analysed earlier. While examples of industrialization, such as that provided by South Korea, demonstrate the importance of such actions, historically the case which shows the greatest degree of state dominance of the process is the Soviet Union. After all, South Korea remained characterized by a capitalist market economy (albeit one that was quite heavily governed) and the direct role of the state was limited by the capitalist character of South Korea's industrialization – there were always going to be limits to what could be done by the state and what would be left to markets. In contrast the communist route followed by the Soviet Union was predicated on the belief that it was the state's role to undertake the key tasks of transition itself. As we noted earlier, the transition to industrial capitalism involves both a process of industrialization and a transition to capitalism. The Soviet route was one where industrialization occurred under a different social system – communism – with a transition to capitalism coming much later (see below).

Industrialization in Russia had begun before the Communist Revolution of 1917 and indeed the small but emerging working class provided the initial backbone of support for the Bolsheviks. However, it was in the aftermath of the revolution and the civil war that followed that the Soviet Union became an industrialized state. You will remember that we have already seen what the communist 'model' entailed when we looked at socialist models of development in Chapter 14 of the Course Book and a quick reminder might be useful now.

Activity 18

Look at Chapter 14 of the Course Book. Make a note of the characteristics of the socialist model that are identified on page 309. What are the key differences between this model and the capitalist route?

Comment

It is clear just from this brief summary that the communist path to industrialization was very different from the transition to industrial capitalism with which we have been concerned up to now. In the capitalist system markets play a central role in shaping the supply of labour to industrial enterprises, the accumulation of savings and the direction of investment into industry, all based on private ownership of the means of production. In the communist model, state ownership replaces private ownership. The state does not just complement and influence market relations but supplants them with administrative 'planning', determining key economic decisions. Furthermore, while one-party rule is certainly not unknown in capitalist countries, it was a central defining feature of Communist states. Let's look at two of the dimensions of this route a bit more closely.

A key element of transition is, as we have seen, the separation of labour from the land, the ending of traditional pre-capitalist social relations and the incorporation and control of labour in the new centres of industrial production. In the Soviet Union the state led this process. Prior to the Communist Revolution in 1917 some significant change had already occurred in agriculture – serfdom had been abolished in the 1860s and a small but growing industrial labour force was already in existence. However, in the aftermath of the revolution, much remained to be done if the country was to industrialize. How was this to be done?

Activity 19

Read Section 14.2 of Chapter 14: 'The dilemmas and contradictions of Soviet socialist development' (pp.310–313 in the Course Book).

Make a few notes summarizing the opposing viewpoints of Bukharin and Preobrazhensky as to how to resolve the land issue.

What was Stalin's response to this question?

(Spend about 15 minutes on this)

Comment

As you will have read, under Stalin's leadership the Communist regime undertook a rapid and forcible re-organization of agriculture. This was done by forcing peasants (who traditionally worked on their own areas of land) into state-owned collective farms, a process known as the 'collectivization of agriculture'. Millions of other peasants were simply forced off the land altogether and relocated to new industrial towns, to the mines, or sent to work on the massive infrastructure projects that the state undertook. This move, enacted between the late 1920s and early 1930s, was accompanied by widespread and brutal political repression of those perceived as political opponents. It was the clearest example of a direct and forcible state-led process of creating an industrial labour force.

The immediate result of the collectivization of agriculture was a catastrophic famine in the Soviet Union caused by the massive disruption which it entailed, the forced relocation of millions of peasants, and peasant opposition to the process in the form of a refusal to supply food to the towns. However, by acting in this direct, if brutal way, the state rapidly 'resolved' one dimension of transition and the urban population increased by 40% between 1928 and 1932 (Kemp, 1983).

But how were other aspects of transition managed by the state, and in particular how did the state ensure that the necessary investment in industry took place? As with labour, so with investment, the state was the crucial actor. As you will have noted in Activities 18 and 19, the centrepiece of the communist command economies was state ownership of enterprises and the central planning of investment (Course Book, p.309). You will have noted the contrast with capitalist systems that this presents. For a start the Soviet system outlawed the private ownership of industrial firms, which meant that investment could not take place on the basis of autonomous decisions by private economic actors. While the state in South Korea did try to influence and participated in industrial investment, in the Soviet Union industrial investment was done by the state.

The key activity in the Soviet approach was the calculation of so-called 'material balances' and the setting of input and output targets for enterprises and collective farms. Thus, in a massive administrative undertaking, the quantities of everything from steel plate and coal to tractor engines and cars to shoes and clothing were set centrally. It has been estimated that up to 48 000 specific targets (or 'plan positions') were set in an attempt to determine the quantities of some 12 million products (Nove, 1983). These targets were set within a rigidly hierarchical system and allocated to individual enterprises. The 'five-year plans' within which these targets were set had to try to ensure that if any specific factory was told to produce a certain number of, say, tractors, then enough supplies would also be directed to it to enable it to fulfil the plan, which in turn meant setting targets for all the supply industries. The scale and complexity of the undertaking made it cumbersome and massively bureaucratic.

However, it did allow a powerful role for the state in determining the overall direction of economic growth, which in turn created a powerful tool consciously to promote the industrialization of the whole society. The emphasis was put on the development of heavy industry – coal, iron and steel and heavy manufacturing such as shipbuilding as well as (and partly because of) the priority given to production of goods for the military. Consequently, in the Soviet Union there was a massive rise in the investment share of GDP relative to consumption and to agriculture and a rapid growth of industry was indeed achieved. As Chapter 14 of the Course Book noted, industrialization meant that the Soviet Union was able to withstand Nazi invasion in the Second World War and to rival the United States during the Cold War.

In the Soviet Union the state almost totally supplanted markets in crucial areas of transition and became the crucial agency in the process. The rapidity of Soviet industrialization and its apparent early success are testament to the potential for the state to achieve fundamental changes in society albeit at enormous social and human cost. The Soviet economy was transformed from a mainly agricultural one into an industrial superpower and became a hugely influential model for others. As Chapter 14 of the Course Book noted (p.311), Trotsky (one of the leaders of the revolution) had argued that the Soviet route was necessary for any country that sought to industrialize, was underdeveloped and dominated by 'imperialism'. Its success led many developing countries, who saw themselves as being in a somewhat similar position to pre-revolutionary Russia, to adopt 'state planning' as a key component of deliberate efforts to undergo transition. Even though few were committed to communism as such and did not develop the kind of all-encompassing state control that the Soviet Union did, nevertheless, in many places in the developing world, states directly took over production processes in key industries, forced labour to relocate away from the land, and sought to direct investment to the industrial sector.

The Soviet experience therefore represents an alternative example of transition to industrialization predicated on the development of an alternative to a transition to capitalism. The *role of the state* was the crucial component of this alternative and the case is useful for us in demonstrating some of the things that action by state authority can achieve. However, it was an inherently limited system. While it proved adept at increasing the levels of production of particular sectors, particularly heavy industry and capital goods, it proved much less able to determine the quality of products or to develop consumer goods industries. Chronic shortages of basic goods for consumers and of inputs for manufacturing industries were an endemic feature of the Soviet economy. It is one thing to create a plan which sets out the numbers of tractors to be produced: it is quite another to specify successfully that they should be good quality tractors. Furthermore, promoting technological advance proved to be something that was beyond the state planning system to deliver, at least outside of the military sector which received massive resource inputs and faced competition from the military sectors of other states. The system was unable to create incentives for innovation which, as we saw in Section 2.2, is a crucial component in allowing industrialization to deliver sustained high growth rates. Indeed, growth in the Soviet economy stagnated in the 1970s and 1980s and increasingly lost ground to the capitalist world outside the Communist block.

By the mid-1980s the Soviet leadership opted to try to reform the system, largely by reducing the directive role of the state and allowing some of the 'freedoms' (economic and political) seen as more characteristic of capitalism. Although intended as a way to reinvigorate the Soviet system, the reforms initiated by Mikhail Gorbachev's leadership undermined the control exercised by the state (see p.317 of the Course Book for a summary of these changes). By the late 1980s signs that the authorities would not use force to maintain control led to widespread popular protests against the communist system which rapidly disintegrated – first, in 1989, in Eastern Europe, and culminating in 1991 in the break-up of the Soviet Union itself.

The road that the Communist states then embarked on was a new transition – that from a state-controlled communist system to capitalism. It is worth noting briefly some of the key elements of this. Transition from communism to capitalism involves precisely those features which distinguished the two systems which we noted in Activity 18:

- The creation of private property in the place of state-ownership of the means of production.
- The creation of markets for labour, capital and goods and services in the place of state allocation of resources.
- The political liberalization of the state itself in the place of communist one-party control.

This process of transition from plan to market has proved to be a problematic and complex process with which the former Soviet Union and much of Eastern Europe are still struggling. However, what we should note is that the key elements of it involve transformations in the relationship of the state to the economy – precisely those relationships that defined the communist route to industrialization. And while the leaders of the Soviet Union certainly did not perceive it this way, in hindsight the Soviet example can be seen to have turned out to have been a transition in which there was first state-led industrialization and subsequently a transition to capitalism in which the role of the state is restructured.

So what does our discussion so far tell us about the role of the state in the transition to industrial capitalism? Apart from anything else we have noted a variety of kinds of actions that the state can undertake.

Activity 20

Think back over the preceding discussion and Section 3 on markets. Make a note of the different ways in which the state can be involved in communist and capitalist transitions.

(Spend about 15 minutes on this)

Comment

You will probably have noted that the kinds of actions taken by the state vary a great deal. In market economies we noted how the state is important for ensuring property rights and in providing the framework necessary to make markets possible.

In South Korea, the state took a more active role in:

■ governing the market,

■ creating incentives for investment to be directed towards export industries, and

■ undertaking reforms in agriculture that helped to create an industrial labour force.

In the Soviet Union we see some similar areas of activity – labour and investment – but undertaken in a way that means that the state replaces markets rather than acting to create, complement and govern markets. The subsequent transition to capitalism in the Soviet Union has seen the state liberalizing and privatizing the economy in a problematic attempt to create markets and private property.

We have therefore established that the state is a powerful and important agency in processes of transition and that the role of this agency can vary a great deal. But why is the state such a potent force in societies in transition? How is the state able to act in the ways we have identified and why does it do so? To address these issues we need to ask some deeper questions about states: what do we mean by 'the state'? What is it about states that make them such an important agency in transition? What are the means at the state's disposal to play a role in transitions? How do we understand the relationship between the state and the society over which it rules? We will be looking at these questions in the following subsection.

4.2 What are states, what do they do and how do they do it?

Let us begin by asking the most obvious question: what do we mean by 'the state'?

Activity 21

One way to approach this question is to identify the 'key features' of states. Go back to Chapter 9 of the Course Book and re-read pp.190–192 of Thomas and Allen's chapter on agencies of development. Make a list summarizing the key features of states identified there.

Comment

Some of the key features that are mentioned are as follows:

■ Each state claims the right to regulate internal affairs and provide security from external threats.

■ The state claims a monopoly on the use of force within its boundaries.

■ The state seeks predominance over other organizations and actors.

■ A state is a set of institutions and bureaucracies that is wider than, and distinct from, government.

Indeed, these features are often cited in attempts to define 'the state'. One such definition that you might find useful is given by the British political scientist David Held, when he writes that states are:

> ... political apparatuses, distinct from both ruler and ruled, with supreme jurisdiction over a demarcated territorial area, backed by a claim to a monopoly of coercive power, and enjoying legitimacy as a result of a minimum level of support or loyalty from their citizens.
>
> (Held, 1995, p.48)

Let us unpack this definition.

■ States are 'political apparatuses', that is, they are concerned with politics. We can usefully define politics as 'collectively binding decision-making'. Given that states are apparatuses ruling over entire societies, then they are apparatuses through which collectively binding decision-making of society takes place and through which those decisions are upheld in society. Note that 'collectively binding decisions' does *not* imply that everyone has a say in such decisions or that they are democratic – merely that they apply to the collective (society).

■ States are 'distinct from both ruler and ruled'. At first glance this may appear somewhat strange – isn't a ruler of a society also (literally) 'the head of state'? What is meant by this relates to point 4 of Thomas and Allen's list of 'features' – that the state is not coterminous with society – it is an identifiable and distinct entity *within* society. It is thus distinct from the ruled – the society over which it exercises jurisdiction. Furthermore, the state exists independent of any individual or set of individuals – it continues to exist even if particular office holders, members of government and heads of state come and go. And their political power, while they have it, is due to their occupancy of positions of office in the state, it is not due to their personal characteristics.

■ The state also has 'supreme jurisdiction over a demarcated territorial area'. The state is thus the final authority and the highest law-making body, seeking predominance over others within society and independence from those without. This rule is exercised over a demarcated territory – within the physical borders of a state.

■ This claim to supremacy is backed by 'a claim to a monopoly of coercive power' – the use of state agencies such as the army and police force to uphold the decisions of the state.

■ Finally, the state, if its rule is to be consolidated and stable, must also enjoy a minimum level of legitimacy and some loyalty and support from the citizenry – an issue we return to below. It must also be accepted as a state (and its right to rule over a specific territory must be accepted) by other states in the world.

We should note three further things here.

First, the definition given is of the 'modern' state. Several of these features would not be found in pre-modern or traditional states. For example, the separation of the state from the ruler was not a feature of absolute monarchies in Europe (roughly sixteenth to eighteenth centuries) when state power was embodied in the king or queen. The demarcated territories over which a state exercises rule is also something that many pre-modern societies do not have where jurisdictions overlapped and the right to rule over particular territories was ill-defined and more complex. For our purposes, in assessing the role of the state in industrialization, this definition of a modern state will suffice as those states that have presided over industrialization have been modern, or at least in some sense *modernizing*, states.

Secondly, the realization of these 'ideal' features of 'statehood' in any one state is always in question (something we discuss further, below).

Finally, each state exists not in isolation but in a state system comprising many other states. Relations between states are often crucial to understanding the emergence, existence and stability of any individual state.

In analysing transitions, when we ask 'what do states do?' we are talking of particular instances in which the state seeks to uphold collectively binding decisions that have some impact on the transition process. We noted in our comments for Activity 20 above that in both the South Korean and Soviet cases there are a variety of such actions. What sense can we make of these? One question we can ask is: what is the *scope* of state actions? States may rule over a highly limited area of social life – defining property rights, defending the territory and regulating violence within the state as well as providing necessary functional needs of the economy such as a stable currency, public goods and certain essential forms of regulation. These kinds of activities are characteristic of capitalist states and are precisely the sorts of things that neoliberals think the state *should* be confined to (see pp.42–45 of the Course Book for a discussion of neoliberalism). Alternatively, states may have a more expansive realm of action, including:

■ provision of social welfare to the population;

■ regulation of aspects of family and personal life;

■ regulation of trade and other economic exchanges beyond the state's borders;

■ undertaking directly certain economic activities – including production in some sectors of the economy.

In both senses, the state can be both a complement to the market (providing some of the institutional setting in which markets exist). At times, it may also be a rival, replacing the market with direct authoritative allocation. Such activity within a capitalist context includes some of the kinds of things that the South Korean state engaged in, in order to promote the country's transition. Finally, as the Soviet case demonstrates, the state can also expand the scope of action to try to determine almost any area of social activity: production, distribution, investment, the use of labour, political and cultural life and so on.

Indeed, this scope of action was one of the crucial things which we noted as distinguishing the communist from capitalist routes to industrialization.

From our definition of what a state is, we can also see why the state is such a distinctive and important agency in transition. The state has considerable means at its disposal to effect change in society. We noted that the state claims a monopoly on the use of **force** within its territory and the use of force, or the threat of it, is one clear means by which a state can act. We noted above how the forcible removal of people from the land was often one component in the creation of labour markets. The state is the only body which claims exclusive jurisdiction over a territory and is the **law**-making authority in a society – there are no other agencies within, outside or above the state that claim a superior authority to make laws. And the state, by virtue of its powers to set taxes and raise revenues, to define laws and use force, is in a unique position to create **incentives** to certain kinds of action.

> **Force:** Coercion or compulsion, especially with the use or threat of violence.
>
> **Law:** A rule in a community or society compelling or proscribing certain actions and enforced by the imposition of penalties.
>
> **Incentive:** A motive or inducement to action.

Activity 22

The above has been a fairly abstract discussion of states. Make sure that you are able to answer the following questions. If you have difficulties, re-read Section 4.2 up to this point. You don't have to write any notes here if you don't need to – just ensure that you can answer the questions.

(a) Explain Held's definition of *a state*.

(b) Explain what is meant by saying that *a state's actions can vary in scope*.

(c) Why are states such distinct agencies in the transition process?

(Spend 10–15 minutes on this)

So far so good: states are important agencies in the transition process due to their unique characteristics. Historically, they have used this ability to act in different ways in different transition processes. However, states are important to transitions for another reason and that is because transitions typically entail a structural change in the way that societies are ruled. The breakdown of traditional social relations – the relations that tied peasants to the land in pre-industrial Europe, Korea or Russia for example – also involved a breakdown of the way that those subordinate social groups were ruled. In rather simplified terms, a traditional right to farm a particular area of land was often bound up with various obligations and a politically subordinate relationship to a landlord. As this pattern of social relations unravels with the movement of labour off the land, the 'political' side also comes apart. Large numbers of people are freed politically as well as economically from traditional ties. Transition thus entails some kind of reconstitution of how society is ruled – in concrete terms, how order can be maintained in societies where masses of individuals have been uprooted from pre-industrial social relations. The promotion of transition by the state (by encouraging this movement off the land, for example) also necessitates that the relationship between the state and those over whom it rules be recreated. Transition to industrial capitalism is thus not simply a process of thunderous economic and social change but of political change too. A crucial part of this is how the state is able to maintain order and stability. Sometimes states fail in this task: the Russian Revolution was in part the result of the fact that the Tsarist state could not control the transition to industrial capitalism in pre-revolutionary Russia (as well as its effective defeat in the First World War).

Legitimacy and power

In the foregoing text we are implicitly acknowledging that the state is involved in a **power** relationship with society. States typically have *power over* others defined as 'the ability to get others to act in a way that is different from how they would otherwise have acted' and *power to do* certain things. These distinctions were noted in *Study Guide 1* (Activities 40–42). They are evident in what we have said about states – the Soviet state moving peasants off the land into factories or the South Korean state trying to ensure that investment goes into certain industries and not others, for example. As *Study Guide 1* noted, power does not have to be overt and can just as effectively operate in hidden ways. However, power necessarily refers to a relationship between actors – and the citizens of a state may be able to exert some power over states to restrict or modify what they do. The political struggles to modify the operation of the labour market, which we noted in Section 3, would be an example of this. Thus a state's role in transition processes is a contested one and the way in which a state's ability to rule is upheld is also contested. In many ways this is true of states anywhere at any time. But the social tumult involved in transitions exacerbates these tensions.

> **Power:** The ability to get others to act in a way that is different from how they would otherwise have acted.

This fact was acknowledged in the Course Book when in Chapters 2 (p.41) and 9 (p.189) it is noted that states *claim* the *right* to impose their will and pursue activities to *try* to ensure they have the *ability* (or might) to impose their will. These comments alert us to the contested nature of state rule – they *claim* certain things and *try to do* certain things. Indeed, each dimension of the definition given above is open to challenge:

- the supreme jurisdiction claimed by a state may be challenged by other bodies or actors claiming to make laws;
- the territory may be subject to challenges from without (invasion) or from within (secession);
- the claim to a monopoly of the use of force may be challenged by armed groups within and without of the state;
- the claim to legitimacy, to which we come in a moment, is always open to dissent.

If the state also tries to engage in economic activity in a direct way it is also likely to be open to challenge. For example, even in the Soviet Union, in which the state had an overbearing presence in society, there were nevertheless repeated instances of resistance by workers to pressure from enterprise managers over working conditions. The state is thus engaged in a constant struggle to consolidate and impose its rule. Furthermore we might note, as Thomas and Allen do in Point 2 of their 'key features of states' (p.190), that part of the distinction between 'strong' and 'weak' states is defined precisely in terms of how successfully the state is able to win the power contest, to achieve predominance and to impose its rule. This is often something of pressing concern to developing countries but we should not assume that such issues of stability are absent from the politics of more developed states too.

One of the key things that ensures the ability of a state to rule, and its strength or weakness, is the extent to which the state's *right* to rule is accepted. This brings us to the question of legitimacy.

Activity 23

Without worrying about whether you are 'correct' or not, write down a few words off the top of your head about what you understand by the term 'legitimate' or 'legitimacy'. Then note what you think makes state power legitimate (or if you prefer a slightly different question, when would you accept the government of a state as legitimate and when not?).

Comment

These are not easy questions and have occupied political theorists for many years! In everyday usage, there are different ways that the term is used but you may have come up with notions such as *legitimate* meaning that something is right; proper; lawful; regular; acceptable and so on. When we come to the state's power over society these are indeed relevant aspects of legitimacy. We might accept a government as legitimate if it has come to power in the 'correct' way, or according to the rules. But what makes the rules legitimate? In liberal democratic countries 'legitimate power' is held by those who have won an election, but rules vary. Under monarchical systems the rules say that power is held by the rightful (legitimate) heir to the throne. To be legitimate, state power has to be held according to rules that are justifiable to the less powerful in order for them to be acceptable. And if we were to assess whether state power in a particular instance was legitimate or not we might want to see some evidence of this acceptability demonstrated by those over whom power is exercised.

Similar considerations led David Beetham to define legitimate power thus:

> Where power is acquired and exercised according to justifiable rules, and with evidence of consent, we call it rightful or legitimate.
>
> (Beetham, 1991, p.3)

Let us unpick this definition a little.

1   It is arguing that power has to conform to established rules. States try to legitimate their rule by claiming a legal validity for their power. States which have defined constitutions limit the scope of, and procedure required for, the state to act and are thus an obvious example of power being exercised according to rules. And while it may well be that power is acquired by means other than according to established rules (expropriation, revolutions, coup d'état and so on), nevertheless power-holders generally seek to exercise this power according to some framework of rules if their power is to be consolidated over time.

2   While these rules may vary enormously they have to be justifiable. But justifiable for whom? Beetham argues that the rules have to be justifiable 'in terms of the beliefs and values' of the people over whom the state rules (Beetham, 1991, p.11). That is, the power-holder (the state) has to justify its claim to rule in terms of rules about who can and can't have power. These must be justifiable in terms of what is seen as 'right' by the population as a whole.

3   Legitimation requires some demonstration of the justifiability of the rules by which power is exercised. Such evidence of consent can be manifested through *electoral* activity – for example elections of those in office such as we find in a representative democracy, which not only confers acceptability on the individuals elected but also on the rules by which they are elected; or plebiscites and referendums which are sometimes used by authoritarian regimes to confirm their rule. Or evidence of consent is manifested in *mobilization* – of mass grassroots activity in support of the state – such as we find in some Communist states (Beetham, 1991).

So why is legitimacy so important to states? As we noted above, the degree to which the state can achieve legitimacy is a crucial factor affecting the ability of a state to rule. In this sense recognition of *right* by the population is an important determinant of *ability*. Power that is legitimated is therefore likely to be more effective, stable and orderly than if it is non-legitimate because it will be less open to challenges – it will be seen as more acceptable to the less powerful (Beetham, 1991). In addition, state power in particular is enhanced by legitimacy because the state seeks superiority over other powers in society. States claim supreme jurisdiction within a territory and therefore claim not only to exercise power themselves but also to define the framework for the exercise of all other powers, be they in the workplace, the marketplace, the home or wherever. Legitimating power is thus a particularly pressing concern for states because it has to be at least largely accepted by other sources of power in society (Beetham, 1991, ch.5).

The above discussion can to a large extent be applied to 'the state' in general. However, questions of legitimation are particularly important during transitions because, as we have noted above, the whole way in which a society is ruled may be in flux. It is no coincidence that transitions have often involved great political change – the struggles over the right to vote in nineteenth-century Britain, the removal and subsequent execution of the Tsar in revolutionary Russia in 1917, the military take-over in South Korea – are all examples where existing ways of ruling were challenged. Thus what each of these cases involve (among other things) are conflicts about legitimacy of state power – on what basis can order and rule be (re)established in a way that conforms to rules that are acceptable to the population. The difficulties of this process are amply demonstrated by the way in which order is often imposed in the short term without any legitimacy – the brutal crackdown on peasant opposition in the Soviet Union or military repression in South Korea in the 1960s and 1970s for example. However, in the long term those in power seek ways to find a legitimate basis for their rule, as the move towards democracy in the 1980s in South Korea showed.

We should note one further thing. The rise of industrialization and the processes through which new economic and social relations emerge inherently involve conflicts in which there will be winners and losers. This goes for economic advantages (who gains most from economic growth for example) but also relates to who exercises political power. Transitions therefore often involve the rise of new classes, élites and interests – and the manner in which the state acts and the way that power is exercised by the state is deeply shaped by these. These wider social conflicts also encompass attempts to acquire and legitimate state power.

We therefore need to build into our analysis of transitions these questions of political power and legitimacy. But first let's summarize this subsection.

In this subsection we have:

- defined what states are;
- noted variations in terms of the kinds of actions states may undertake to promote transitions and in the scope of state activity;
- noted how transitions entail the need to reconstitute state power in the context of wide-ranging social change;
- argued that a key part of this is how state power can be legitimated.

4.3 States and transition

The above discussion has brought to our attention the fact that transitions do not just raise questions of the role of the state in processes of structural change but also involve structural change in the relations of political power themselves. This was very clear in the Soviet case with which we began this section.

We noted how the state was a powerful actor able to undertake key aspects of industrialization itself, including the separation of labour from the land and the organization of industrial investment. However, the rise of the Communist state entailed the creation of a new basis for state power. In some respects this was not legitimated in any meaningful way – naked force was used to acquire power (the revolution), to use its power (e.g. collectivization) and to maintain power (continued repression of dissent). There was an attempt to consolidate communist rule on a firmer basis. The claim to legitimacy of the Communist state rested on the claim of the Communist Party to be the leader of the working class, and the claim of the Party that building socialism (of which industrialization was a central component) was the goal of the working class. The victory of the Soviet state in the Second World War (the 'Great Patriotic War' as the Soviets called it) also bolstered the legitimacy of the Communist regime for a time in terms of providing security to the population. As the economy stagnated internally and the gap between living standards under communism and the capitalist world grew ever wider, the legitimacy of the party-state was brought directly into question. For it was the state itself that took the role of organizing the economy on the basis that it could build socialism, which it argued was a superior form of society to capitalism. When it became apparent that the Soviet Union was failing to achieve the kind of continued growth based on innovation, which Section 2 identified as a central feature of intensive growth, it was the state itself, and the form of political rule represented by the leading role of the Communist Party, that was targeted. The rapid collapse of communism, once the use of force by the state was reduced, was testament to the fragility of the state's legitimacy and of the political and economic limitations of this particular route to transition. As we noted above, the result of this was a subsequent period of transition to capitalism. But we should remind ourselves that this latter transition was not just a restructuring of the relationship between state and economy and the creation of markets but of a reconstruction of the entire basis for state rule.

Similarly if we were to take other examples of transition which we have looked at in this *Introduction to Transitions* we can also identify some important aspects of the state's role in transition. We have noted some of the kinds of things that the state did in South Korea already (see Section 3.5 above). But we should also consider the far-reaching conflicts over how the country was ruled in the era of industrialization.

The rise of repressive military government was one 'answer' to the disorder and instability that the rapid process of transition created in the 1950s. The response of the military was not to seek to slow the process of change but to promote it. Industrialization and national development soon became central elements of the military's legitimation of its rule and modernization and industrialization, and later a rising standard of living, were crucial to political stability (Amsden, 1989). By the 1980s even this was not sufficient and a rising tide of opposition to the military paved the way for the gradual move towards a more democratic form of government.

5 Conclusion

In this *Introduction to Transitions* we have sought to understand some of the processes of structural transformation behind the 'thunderous social change' involved in the transition to industrial capitalism. We began by noting how the rise in living standards associated with industrialization was predicated on the achievement of intensive economic growth defined as a rise in GDP per capita over time. This in turn entails structural change in the economy, particularly in the movement of labour away from agriculture. Furthermore, we noted how the advent of capitalism with an increasing division of labour, competition, investment and the pursuit of profit was important to this accelerated rate of growth. We also noted how the role of technology and knowledge in industrial production was important. In Section 3 we analysed the role of markets in the transition process in organizing the mobilization of labour and investment for industrial production. We noted the debate between those who view markets as emerging naturally and those who stress the social creation of markets as institutions. Finally, in Section 4 we saw how the state was a key agency in the transition process and how the importance of the state derived from its unique nature as the pre-eminent apparatus of political power. However, we also investigated how transitions involve a reorganization in the relationship between the state and society and attempts to establish the legitimacy of the state's power.

Activity 24

As a way of concluding your study of *Introduction to Transitions*, try the following activity.

Throughout *Introduction to Transitions* we have mentioned different historical routes to industrial capitalism. We have focused in particular on those followed by Britain in the late eighteenth and nineteenth centuries; the Soviet Union/Russia in the twentieth century; and South Korea in the post-Second World War era.

Identify some key features of each process of transition. You may be able to relate these to the following dimensions:

■ when transition occurred;

■ whether the transition to capitalism occurred before, after, or at more or less the same time as industrialization;

■ how important markets were in driving the process of structural change;

■ how central the state was in the processes of transition, and so on.

(Spend about 20 minutes on this)

As should be clear by this stage, much of what we have looked at in *Introduction to Transitions* addresses one of the key aims of the course – that of 'reframing development'. We have noted already that the distinction between transition to capitalism and transition to industry has important implications for some key debates about conceptions of, and strategies for, development (whether industrialization and/or capitalism are necessary for, or a central aspect of, development). In addition we have seen how unpicking the different processes that make up 'a structural transformation in society as a whole' show the historical importance of economic growth, markets and states in the process of development.

Finally, while this Introduction aims to extend your understanding of development, it also serves as an introduction to the *Transitions* Theme in Part 2 of the course. That part of the course will focus on the 'thunderous social change' currently under way in China. We will therefore be taking some of the processes and concepts that you have studied in *Introduction to Transitions* and deploy them to understand and analyse China's transition.

The *Transitions* Theme in Part 2 begins with a broad historical survey of China in the post-war era before tackling the key processes identified in this Introduction as central to understanding transitions:

- changes in the role and nature of labour and employment;
- changes in property rights and investment, and
- changes in the role of the state and the relationship between the state and society.

As we have indicated, several big issues in development will also arise from the case study and the historical record, nature and potential future direction of China's transition will be debated throughout.

6 *Transitions* Theme, Part 2

The aims and learning outcomes for the *Transitions* Theme in Part 2 are listed below.

Aims

The aims of the *Transitions* Theme, Part 2, are to:

- explore some of the key economic and political processes of the structural transformation of societies entailed in the transition to industrial capitalism;
- introduce some of the key conceptual tools from politics and economics for understanding these processes;
- assess some of the key processes of transition in contemporary China – in particular those relating to changes in: employment and labour; investment and property; and politics and the state – in terms of the nature, extent and potential future direction of transition;
- consider the implications of transitions for reframing development.

Learning outcomes

On completion of Part 2 of the *Transitions* Theme, you should be able to:

Knowledge and understanding

1 Understand some of the key political and economic processes of transitions to industrial capitalism.

2 Understand some of the key conceptual tools drawn from economics and politics in analysing the processes of transition to industrial capitalism.

3 Understand some of the key processes of transition in contemporary China relating in particular to employment and labour; investment and property; and politics and the state.

4 Evaluate the nature of transition in China.

5 Evaluate the implications of transition in China for wider debates about development.

Key skills

6 Communicate ideas and concepts in written material.

7 Apply basic numerical and statistical skills to economic and political data.

8 Interpret and evaluate different sources of data.

Cognitive skills

9   Use some key conceptual tools drawn from economics and politics in analysing the processes of transition to industrial capitalism.

10 Synthesize analysis of discrete processes of change.

11 Use political and economic analysis for analysis of contemporary processes of change.

References

Allen, T. and Thomas, A. (eds.) (2000) *Poverty and Development into the 21st Century*, Oxford University Press, Oxford, in association with the Open University, Milton Keynes [Course Book].

Amsden, A.H. (1989) *Asia's Next Giant: South Korea and late industrialization*, Oxford University Press, New York.

Amsden, A. and Singh, A. (1994) 'The optimal degree of competition and dynamic efficiency in Japan and Korea', *European Economic Review*, vol.38, pp.941–951.

Bairoch, P. (1993) *Economics and World History: myths and paradoxes*, University of Chicago Press, Chicago.

Beetham, D. (1991) *The Legitimation of Power*, Macmillan, Basingstoke.

Cipolla, C.M. (1965) *The Economic History of World Population* (3rd edn), Penguin, Harmondsworth.

Dicken, P. (1998) *Global Shift*, Paul Chapman Publishing Ltd, London.

Easterlin, R.A. (2000) 'The worldwide standard of living since 1800', *The Journal of Economic Perspectives*, vol.14, no.1, Winter 2000, pp.7–26.

Held, D. (1995) *Democracy and the Global Order: from the modern state to cosmopolitan governance*, Stanford University Press, Stanford, CA.

Janelli, R.L. with Yim, D. (1993) *Making Capitalism: the social and cultural construction of a South Korean conglomerate*, Stanford University Press, Stanford, CA.

Jones, E.L. (1988) *Growth Recurring: economic change in world history*, Clarendon Press, Oxford.

Kemp, T. (1983) *Industrialization in the Non-Western World*, Longman, London.

Kornai, J. (2000) 'What the change of system from socialism to capitalism does and does not mean', *The Journal of Economic Perspectives*, vol.14, no.1, pp.27–42.

Landes, D.S. (1999) 'The fable of the dead horse; or, The Industrial Revolution revisited', in Mokyr, J. (ed.), *The British Industrial Revolution: an economic perspective* (2nd edn), pp.128–159, Westview Press, Oxford.

Lie, J. (1998) *Han Unbound: the political economy of South Korea*, Stanford University Press, Stanford, CA.

Maddison, A. (1982) *Phases of Capitalist Development*, Oxford University Press, New York.

Maddison, A. (1991) *Dynamic Forces in Capitalist Development: a long-run comparative view*, Oxford University Press, Oxford.

Maddison, A. (1994) 'Explaining the economic performance of nations, 1820–1989', in Baumol, W.J., Nelson, R.R. and Wolff, E.N. (eds), *Convergence of Productivity: cross-national studies and historical evidence*, pp.20–61, Oxford University Press, New York.

Marx, K. (1970) *Capital: a Critique of Political Economy, Vol.1, Capitalist Production*, Lawrence & Wishart, London. (First published in 1867.)

Mokyr, J. (1999) 'Editor's introduction: the new economic history and the Industrial Revolution', in Mokyr, J. (ed.), *The British Industrial Revolution: an economic perspective* (2nd edn), pp.1–127, Westview Press, Oxford.

Nove, A. (1983) *The Economics of Feasible Socialism*, G. Allen & Unwin, London.

Polanyi, K. (1957) *The Great Transformation: the political and economic origins of our time*, Beacon Press, Boston. (First published in 1944.)

Smith, A. (1993) *An Inquiry into the Nature and Causes of the Wealth of Nations* (selected edn, edited and introduced by Kathryn Sutherland), Oxford University Press, Oxford. (First published in 1776.)

Wade, R. (1990) *Governing the Market: economic theory and the role of government in East Asian industrialization*, Princeton University Press, Princeton, NJ.

World Bank (1993) *The East Asian Economic Miracle*, World Bank, Washington DC.

Wrigley, E.A. (1987) *People, Cities and Wealth: the transformation of traditional society*, Blackwell, Oxford.

Wrigley, E.A. (1988) *Continuity, Chance and Change: the character of the Industrial Revolution in England*, Cambridge University Press, Cambridge.

Acknowledgements

Grateful acknowledgement is made to the following sources for permission to reproduce material within this text.

Tables

Table 2.2: Maddison, A. (1994) 'Explaining the economic performance of nations, 1820–1989', Baumol, W.J., Nelson, R.R. and Wolff, E.N. (eds), *Convergence of Productivity: cross national studies and historical evidence.* Used by permission of Oxford University Press, Inc. © 1982 Angus Maddison; *Table 2.3:* Easterlin, R. A. (2000) 'The worldwide standard of living since 1800', *The Journal of Economic Perspectives,* vol.14, no.1, Winter 2000. American Economic Association; *Tables 2.4 and 2.6:* Maddison, A. (1991) *Dynamic forces in capitalist development.* By permission of Oxford University Press, Inc.; *Table 2.5:* Maddison, A. (1982) *Phases of Capitalist Development.* By permission of Oxford University Press, Inc.; *Table 2.7:* Reprinted by permission of Paul Chapman Publishing Ltd. from Dicken, P. *Global Shift,* Copyright © 1998 Paul Chapman Publishing.

Figures

Figure 2.2: Bradford Delong, J. *Estimating world GDP, one million B.C. – Present.* Reproduced with permission; *Figure 2.3:* Reprinted by permission of Paul Chapman Publishing Ltd. from Dicken, P. *Global Shift,* Copyright © 1998 Paul Chapman Publishing; *Figure 3.1:* © Courtesy of The Karl Polanyi Institute, Concordia University, Montreal, Canada; *Cover photo:* © Tom Hanley.

Every effort has been made to contact copyright owners. If any have been inadvertently overlooked, the publishers will be pleased to make the necessary arrangements at the first opportunity.

The Course Team

ACADEMIC STAFF

Joanna Chataway, *Co-Chair and author, Technology and Knowledge*

Jenny Robinson, *Co-Chair, co-ordinator and author, Displacement*

Gordon Wilson, *Co-Chair, co-ordinator and author, Sustainability*

Simon Bromley, *co-ordinator and author, Transitions*

Will Brown, *co-ordinator and author, Transitions*

Pam Furniss, *author, Sustainability*

Tom Hewitt, *co-ordinator and author, Technology and Knowledge*

Hazel Johnson, *co-ordinator and author, Poverty and Inequality*

Bob Kelly, *assessment strategy and author, Study Guide to the Course Book*

Maureen Mackintosh, *author, Transitions*

Judith Mehta, *author, Transitions*

Stephen Peake, *author, Sustainability*

Sandrine Simon, *author, Sustainability*

Alan Thomas, *author and co-editor of the Course Book*

Richard Treves, *author, Sustainability*

David Wield, *critical reader*

Helen Yanacopulos, *co-ordinator and author, Technology and Knowledge*

BBC STAFF

Jenny Bardwell, *Series Producer July 2000–May 2001*

Gail Block, *Audio Producer*

Giselle Corbett, *Production Manager*

Phil Gauron, *Series Producer*

Julie Laing, *Series Personal Assistant*

Andrew Law, *Executive*

Jenny Morgan, *Freelance Director*

Claire Sandry, *Audio Producer*

Mercia Seminara, *Audio Producer*

SUPPORT STAFF

Carolyn Baxter, *Course Manager*

Sylvan Bentley, *Picture Researcher*

Philippa Broadbent, *Print Buying Controller*

Penny Brown, *QA Software Testing Assistant*

Daphne Cross, *Print Buying Co-ordinator*

Sue Dobson, *Web Designer*

Tony Duggan, *Learning Projects Manager*

Peta Jellis, *Course Manager July–November 2000*

Alison George, *Web Designer*

Richard Hoyle, *Graphic Designer*

Lori Johnston, *Editor*

Roy Lawrance, *Graphic Artist*

Cathy McNulty, *Course Secretary*

Katie Meade, *Rights Editor*

Lynda Oddy, *QA Software Testing Manager*

Pauline O'Dwyer, *Course Secretary*

Katharine Reedy, *Library Online Adviser*

Janice Robertson, *Editor*

John Taylor, *Copublishing Manager*

Mark Thomas, *Team Leader, Online Applications Web Team*

Pamela Wardell, *Editor*

EXTERNAL ASSESSOR

Dr K. Bezanson, *Institute of Development Studies, University of Sussex*

CONSULTANTS

Tim Allen, *author and co-editor of the Course Book*

Seife Ayele, *Poverty and Inequality*

Jo Beall, *Sustainability*

Flemming Christiaansen, *Transitions*

Ben Crow, *Sustainability*

Vandana Desai, *Displacement, and Study Guide to the Course Book*

Wendy Fisher, *Technology and Knowledge*

Leroi Henry, *Study Guide to the Course Book*

Ann Le Mare, *Preparing for Development*

Giles Mohan, *Displacement*

Paul Mosley, *Poverty and Inequality*

Njuguna N'gethe, *Study Guide to the Course Book*

Wendy Olsen, *Poverty and Inequality*

Ruth Pearson, *Poverty and Inequality*

Judith Scott, *Poverty and Inequality*

Laixiang Sun, *Transitions*

John Taylor, *Transitions*

David Turton, *Displacement*

Marc Wuyts, *Transitions*

CRITICAL READERS

Henry Bernstein, *Transitions*

Tenkai Bonger, *Sustainability*

Jessimen Chipika, *Poverty and Inequality*

Rachel Marcus, *Poverty and Inequality*

Martin Reynolds, *Sustainability*

Rafal Rohozinski, *Technology and Knowledge*

AbdouMaliq Simone, *Displacement*

WEB TESTERS

Alan Brown, Jackie Bush, Christine Cubbitt, Andrew Dakers, Sarah Downham, Alan Foster, Anna Mattarollo, Fahmida Muhit, Eric Needs, Wendy Shaffer, Nigel Shakespear, Phil Talman

U213
International Development: Challenges for a World in Transition

Course texts

Introduction to Transitions

Introduction to Poverty and Inequality

Introduction to Technology and Knowledge

Introduction to Displacement

Introduction to Sustainability

Transitions

Poverty and Inequality

Technology and Knowledge (web-based)

Displacement

Sustainability